Evil Under the Sun

Agatha Christie

D1340509

Level 4

Retold by Liz Kilbey

Series Editors: Andy Hopkins and Jocelyn Potter

989900391105 4X

Pearson Education Limited

Edinburgh Gate, Harlow,
Essex CM20 2JE, England
and Associated Companies throughout the world.

Pack ISBN: 978-1-4082-3204-0

This edition first published by Pearson Education Ltd 2010

1 3 5 7 9 10 8 6 4 2

Text copyright © Pearson Education Ltd 2010

AGATHA CHRISTIE* POIROT* Copyright © 2009
Agatha Christie Limited (a Chorion company). All rights reserved.
Evil Under the Sun Copyright © 1941 Agatha Christie Limited.
All rights reserved.

Illustrations by Patrick Morgan at Début Art

The moral rights of the authors have been asserted in accordance
with the Copyright Designs and Patents Act 1988

Set in 11/13pt A. Garamond

Printed in China
SWTC/01

Published by Pearson Education Ltd in association with Penguin Books Ltd,
both companies being subsidiaries of Pearson PLC

For a comp   :ries please
write to your local Pearson Longman office or to: Penguin Readers Marketing Department,
Pearson Education, Edinburgh Gate, Harlow, Essex CM20 2JE, England.

Contents

1.1 What's the book about?

1 Have you read other books by Agatha Christie, or seen any films of her stories? Who were the main characters? What happened in the stories? Discuss the kind of books that she wrote.

2 Read the descriptions of six characters in the story. Then guess who the people in the pictures are. Write their names under the pictures.

a .... b .... c ....

d .... e .... f ....

1 Patrick Redfern is a tall, sporty young man who is very attractive to women.

2 Kenneth Marshall is a quiet, shy, loyal man.

3 Horace Blatt is a loud, red-faced man who other people find boring.

4 Arlena Marshall is a beautiful young woman who enjoys the company of men.

5 Hercule Poirot is a clever middle-aged Belgian detective.

6 Linda Marshall is a shy, embarrassed teenager.

1.2 What happens first?

Look at the titles and pictures in the first two chapters. Do you think these sentences are true (T) or false (F)?

1 Hercule Poirot is on holiday at the hotel.   ....

2 The hotel is usually full of noisy holiday-makers.   ....

3 The main characters in the story work at the hotel.   ....

4 One female character is disliked by all the other women.   ....

5 Many of the characters have secrets.   ....

CHAPTER 1

A Quiet Hotel

'The sun shines. The sea is blue. But, Miss Brewster,
there is evil everywhere under the sun.'

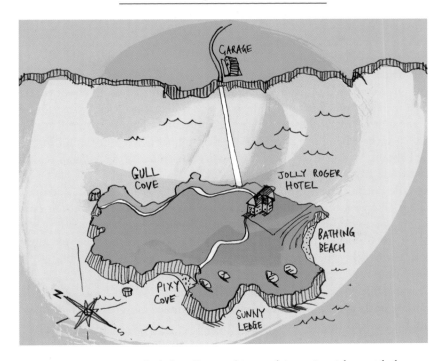

Hercule Poirot was on holiday. Dressed in a white suit with a wide hat protecting his eyes, his handsome moustache carefully styled, he looked down at the beach. He was staying at the Jolly Roger Hotel on **Smugglers'** Island, on the south-west coast of England. It was a very comfortable hotel and very quiet. Not many day visitors made their way to the island, which was completely separated from the **mainland** at every high **tide**.

On the beach, some people were in the sea, while others were lying in the sun. Next to Poirot, hotel guests were discussing all kinds of subjects. On his left Mrs Gardener was **knitting** while she talked. Her husband Odell spoke

smuggler /ˈsmʌɡələ/ (n) someone who takes things illegally from one country to another
mainland /ˈmeɪnlænd, -lənd/ (n) the main area of land that forms a country; not the islands near it
tide /taɪd/ (n) the regular movement of the sea, towards the land (*high tide*) and away from the land (*low tide*)
knit /nɪt/ (v) to make clothes with wool, using special long needles

1

only when a reply seemed to be expected. On Poirot's right was Miss Brewster, a strong, fit woman whose pleasant face had been aged by time spent outdoors.

'Odell and I have seen England now,' said Mrs Gardener, 'and we just wanted to relax somewhere by the sea. Isn't that right, dear?' Her husband, from behind his sun hat, agreed. 'We were looking for somewhere away from the crowds, and, well, special. We were very pleased when we found this place. It's full of such interesting people. You, for example, Monsieur* Poirot. I was so excited when I discovered who you were – wasn't I, Odell?'

'Yes, dear.'

'I've always wanted to meet you. Cornelia Robson told us all about that business in Egypt when Linnet Ridgeway was killed. And there's Miss Darnley too. I get a lot of my clothes from Rose Mond's, and of course she *is* Rose Mond, isn't she? I was wearing one of her dresses last night. There's just one thing I'm worried about, Monsieur Poirot. I hope you're not here for *professional* reasons? I'd hate to be anywhere near a crime …'

Hercule Poirot threw his hands up into the air. 'I promise you, Madame, that I am here, like you, to enjoy myself. I am not even going to think about crime.'

'There are no bodies on *this* island!' Miss Brewster laughed.

'Ah,' replied Poirot, 'but that is not quite true. Look at those people, down there on the beach. They are not men and women. They are just – bodies!'

'And some very attractive ones too!' added **Major** Barry.

'Perhaps, but where is the mystery?' asked Poirot. 'When I was young, one saw almost nothing of a woman's body. The romance has gone. In fact, they remind me of dead bodies – or pieces of meat.'

'Oh, Monsieur Poirot!' cried Mrs Gardener, shocked. 'But I agree that the girls shouldn't lie in the sun like that. They'll grow hair all over their bodies, and then what will they look like? I told my daughter that, didn't I, Odell?'

'Yes, dear,' Mr Gardener replied.

Everyone was silent, perhaps imagining the Gardeners' daughter when the worst had happened. Mrs Gardener put away her knitting, and she and her husband made their way towards the hotel. The others watched them.

'American husbands are wonderful!' said Miss Brewster.

Mrs Gardener's place was taken by **Reverend** Stephen Lane. He was a tall man in his fifties, wearing informal holiday clothes.

'A wonderful area!' he said. 'I've been for a walk along the **cliffs**.'

---

* Monsieur, Madame, Mademoiselle: the French words for Mr/sir, Mrs/madam and Miss

Major /ˈmeɪdʒə/ (n) the title of an officer in the British army

Reverend /ˈrevərənd/ (n) a title used for some officials of the Christian church

cliff /klɪf/ (n) high land with a very steep side next to the sea

'Ah, that's good exercise!' replied Miss Brewster. 'I haven't been **rowing** yet today. It's a good way to keep one's stomach flat.' Hercule Poirot's eyes dropped uncomfortably to his rather large waist. Noticing his look, Miss Brewster said kindly, 'That would soon disappear, Monsieur Poirot, if you took a rowing-boat out each day.'

'*Non, merci!** I hate boats! The movement of the sea is not pleasant.'

'Seasickness is very odd, isn't it?' said Miss Brewster. 'Why should some people suffer and not others? It's the same with heights. I don't like them, but Mrs Redfern suffers much more. A few days ago on the cliff path she got quite faint and had to hold onto me. She told me she's always had problems.'

'She'd better not go down the ladder to Pixy **Cove**, then,' said Lane. 'Ah, here she comes now,' he added. 'She's finished her swim.'

Christine Redfern was drying her hair as she walked towards them. She had very pale skin.

'She isn't as cooked as the others, is she?' Major Barry said, laughing loudly.

* *Non, merci!*: French for *No, thank you!*

row /rəʊ/ (v) to move a boat through water using special long pieces of shaped wood
cove /kəʊv/ (n) part of the coast where the land curves and partly surrounds the sea

Christine Redfern climbed the steps towards them and dropped down into one of the chairs. Miss Brewster turned to her.

'You have earned Monsieur Poirot's good opinion,' she said. 'He doesn't like people who lie in the sun. He thinks they look like pieces of meat.'

'I'd *like* to be able to lie in the sun!' smiled Christine, pushing back her hair with a small, white hand. 'But I don't go brown. My skin just burns.'

'That's better than becoming hairy, like Mrs Gardener's daughter,' said Miss Brewster. Christine looked at her. 'Mrs Gardener's been talking all morning. Why didn't you tell her, though, Monsieur Poirot, that you were working on a terrible murder, and that the murderer was certainly one of the hotel guests?'

Poirot looked serious. 'I fear that she would believe me if I did that.'

Emily Brewster disagreed. 'Not even Mrs Gardener would believe that there could be a crime here. This isn't the sort of place you'd find a body!'

'Why not, Mademoiselle? True, Smugglers' Island is a romantic place. It is peaceful. The sun shines. The sea is blue. But, Miss Brewster, there is **evil** everywhere under the sun.'

Stephen Lane moved forwards in his chair. His blue eyes shone.

'You forget one thing, Mademoiselle,' continued Poirot.

'Human nature?'

'Yes, certainly. But I was going to say that here everyone is on holiday.'

Emily Brewster looked confused. 'I don't understand.'

Poirot smiled kindly. 'Let us imagine that you have an enemy. If you look for him in his flat, in his office, in the street, you must have a *reason* for being there. But here at the seaside, you do not need to explain anything. It is August – one goes to the seaside in August. It is quite natural for you to be here.'

'But what about the Gardeners? They're American.'

Poirot smiled. 'Even Mrs Gardener, as she told us, feels the need to *relax*. Also, since she is touring England, she must spend a couple of weeks at the seaside – as a good tourist. And Mrs Gardener enjoys watching people.'

'*You* like watching people, I think?' said Mrs Redfern quietly.

'Madame, that is true, I do.'

She said thoughtfully, 'You see – a lot.'

For a moment, there was silence. Then Stephen Lane spoke.

'You said, Monsieur Poirot, that evil was done everywhere under the sun. The Bible says, *The hearts of men are full of evil, and madness is in their hearts while they live.* These days, not many people believe in evil. But, Monsieur Poirot, evil is *real*. It is a *fact*. It is powerful!' The reverend stopped suddenly and looked embarrassed. 'I'm sorry,' he said. 'I get too excited.'

evil /ˈiːvəl/ (n/adj) a power that makes people do very bad things; very cruel behaviour

'I understand,' said Poirot, 'and I agree that evil is real.'

'This reminds me of when I was in India …' Major Barry began, but both Miss Brewster and Mrs Redfern quickly interrupted him.

'That's your husband over there in the sea, isn't it, Mrs Redfern?' cried Miss Brewster. 'He's a very good swimmer.'

'Oh, look!' said Christine Redfern, at the same time. 'What a lovely little boat, with the red sails! It's Mr Blatt's, isn't it?'

Hercule Poirot looked with admiration at the young man who had just swum back to the beach. Patrick Redfern was a handsome, fit young man with a cheerful, relaxed personality that all women and most men found attractive.

Christine waved and called to him, 'Come up here, Pat.'

'I'm coming!' he replied, turning to pick up his towel.

Just then, a woman came down past them from the hotel to the beach. Her arrival had a great effect, and she seemed to know it. She was tall and beautiful with red-brown hair falling to her neck. She was wearing a simple white swimsuit and her body was perfectly **tanned**. On her head she wore an unusual Chinese sun hat, made of dark green **cardboard**. Every other woman on the beach suddenly looked dull. Every man's eyes were watching her.

Hercule Poirot's eyes opened too. Major Barry sat up straighter in his chair. Stephen Lane breathed in deeply.

'Arlena Stuart!' the major said. 'Arlena *Marshall*, since her marriage. I saw her in *Come and Go*, before she stopped acting. Good to look at, isn't she!'

'She's good-looking, yes,' Christine Redfern replied slowly and coldly, 'but I think she looks rather … unpleasant.'

Emily Brewster spoke. 'You were talking about evil, Monsieur Poirot. In my opinion, that woman is evil. I know a lot about her.'

'She reminds me of a girl I knew in India,' said Major Barry. 'She had red hair too. Men were crazy about her, but her husband never seemed to notice.'

'Women like that are dangerous,' said Stephen Lane. 'They're …'

He stopped. Arlena Marshall was standing on the beach. Two young men had jumped up and were moving towards her. She smiled at them, but then her eyes turned towards Patrick Redfern. He stopped and it appeared, thought Poirot, that his feet were not under his control. They carried him towards her.

Arlena moved slowly along the beach and lay down beside a rock. Patrick sat down next to her. Christine stood up suddenly and walked back to the hotel.

There was an uncomfortable silence, then Emily Brewster spoke.

'How sad. She's so nice. They've only been married for a year or two.'

tan /tæn/ (v/n) to get darker skin from spending time in the sun
cardboard /ˈkɑːdbɔːd/ (n/adj) very thick paper, especially used for making boxes

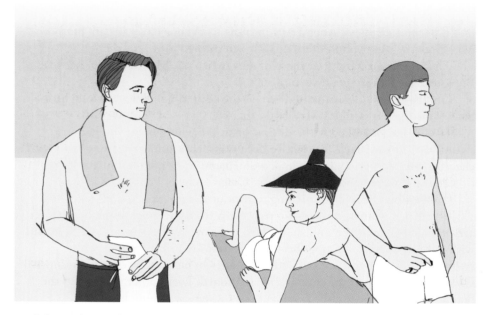

'The girl in India destroyed two marriages,' said Major Barry.

'Some women,' said Miss Brewster, 'enjoy that. Patrick Redfern's a fool!'

Hercule Poirot said nothing. He was watching the beach, but he was not looking at Arlena Stuart and Patrick Redfern.

Emily Brewster stood up. 'It's time for me to go rowing.'

When she had gone, Major Barry turned to Poirot. 'Well, Poirot, what do you think of the girl? I know you Frenchmen like beautiful women!'

'I am *not* a Frenchman!' replied Poirot angrily. 'Yes, she is beautiful, but I am looking at the only person whose head did *not* turn to look at her.'

Major Barry looked down to where Poirot was pointing. A man of about forty, with a quiet, pleasant face, was sitting on the beach. He was smoking a **pipe** and reading a newspaper.

'Oh! That's her husband. He seems a nice man. Quiet. Well, I wonder if my newspaper has arrived yet.' Major Barry got up and walked towards the hotel.

Stephen Lane was watching Arlena and Patrick. He suddenly turned to Poirot. 'That woman is completely evil. Do you agree?'

'It's difficult to be sure,' Poirot replied slowly.

'But don't you feel it in the air? All around you? Evil!'

Slowly, Hercule Poirot **nodded** his head.

pipe /paɪp/ (n) a tube with a bowl-shaped container at one end, used for smoking tobacco

nod /nɒd/ (v) to move your head up and down to show understanding or agreement

CHAPTER 2

Private Conversations

She hadn't realised until now how much she disliked Arlena.
'She's horrible,' she thought, 'horrible …'

Rosamund Darnley came and sat down next to Hercule Poirot, who looked pleased. He admired her greatly. She was, he thought, a most attractive woman, with a pleasant smile.

'I don't think I like this place!' said Rosamund, 'I'm wondering why I came!'

'Has something happened that's worrying you?' Hercule Poirot asked gently.

She nodded, and stared down at her feet. 'I've met a ghost,' she said.

'Whose ghost, Mademoiselle?'

'My own. It was very painful. It brought back memories …' She paused. 'Memories of my childhood.'

'Was it a very English childhood?'

'Oh yes! A big old house in the country, with horses, dogs and walks in the rain. Not enough money, no new clothes …'

'And you want to go back?' asked Poirot gently.

Rosamund Darnley shook her head. 'One can never do that, but I wish …'

'But many people must be jealous of you, Mademoiselle,' said Poirot.

'Oh, yes. Of course.' Rosamund Darnley was amused. 'I'm the perfect, successful woman! I'm an artist and a businesswoman. I sell a lot of my clothes – I'm quite rich, I'm attractive and I'm not too nasty. But, of course, I haven't got a husband. I've failed in that, haven't I, Monsieur Poirot?'

'Mademoiselle,' replied Poirot, 'if you are not married, it is because no man has found the right words. You are single from choice, not necessity.'

'But I am sure you, like all men, believe that no woman is happy unless she's married and has children.'

Poirot disagreed. 'Ordinary women do that. Only one woman in a hundred – no, a thousand – can become famous and successful, as you have done.'

'But I'm still just an old unmarried woman.' Rosamund smiled. 'Well, that's how I feel today: I'd be happier if I were poor, with a husband and children. But of course I have a good life really, and I know it!'

'Then everything is good, Mademoiselle,' said Poirot. After a moment, he continued, 'So, Mr Marshall is an old friend, Mademoiselle?'

Rosamund sat up. 'How do you know that? I suppose he told you?'

'Nobody has told me anything. You forget, I am a detective. You have been here for a week. At first, you were happy and without worries, but today you started speaking about ghosts. What happened today? Mr Marshall arrived with his wife and daughter. It is clear!'

'Well, it's true,' said Rosamund. 'Kenneth Marshall and I were children together. We were neighbours. He was always nice to me, although he's four years older. I haven't seen him for about fifteen years.'

'A long time,' said Poirot. 'He is a nice person, I think?'

'Kenneth's a lovely man. Very quiet and shy. His only fault is that he marries unwisely. Do you remember the Martingdale murder?'

'Martingdale? Martingdale? It was poison, wasn't it?'

'Yes. Seventeen or eighteen years ago. The woman was **suspected** of murdering her husband. But the court decided she was innocent. Well, after that Kenneth married her. That's the kind of silly thing he does!'

'But why not, if she was innocent?' asked Poirot.

'Oh, I'm sure she *was* innocent. But there are plenty of women to marry who haven't been suspected of murder. Of course he was very young – just twenty-one. He was crazy about her. She died when Linda was born, a year after their marriage. Kenneth was very upset, and he behaved rather wildly afterwards, to forget. Then came Arlena Stuart. She was performing in a show at the time. Lord Codrington's wife **divorced** him because he was in love with Arlena, but then he didn't marry her. *Kenneth* married her. The fool!'

'But perhaps we can excuse such behaviour,' said Poirot. 'She is beautiful.'

suspect /səˈspekt/ (v) to believe that someone has done something wrong; this feeling is a *suspicion*

divorce /dɪˈvɔːs/ (v/n) to end a marriage legally

'Yes, there's no doubt about that,' said Rosamund. 'Then there was another big story about three years ago. Old Sir Roger Erskine died, and left Arlena all his money. Surely that was a warning to Kenneth!'

'And wasn't it?'

'I don't know. I told you, I haven't seen him for years. But did he really not mind? Does he love her so much?'

'There might be other reasons,' said Poirot.

'Yes! He's a proud man. He doesn't like showing his feelings. I don't know what he feels for her. Nobody does.'

'And what about her? What does she feel about him, do you think?'

'She's just interested in his money! And she enjoys catching men,' said Rosamund. 'She wants Patrick Redfern now. He's good-looking and fond of his wife – that's Arlena's type of man. I like little Mrs Redfern – she's quite pretty – but she hasn't got a chance against Arlena the man-eater!'

Poirot looked upset. 'No – you are right,' he agreed.

'Christine Redfern was a teacher, I believe. She thinks that brains are more important than appearance. wShe's going to have a shock. It's a pity.'

◆

Linda Marshall was examining her face in the bedroom mirror. She disliked her face very much. She looked unhappily at her soft brown hair, her green-grey eyes, her rather long chin. Her mouth and teeth weren't quite as bad, but was that a spot on the side of her nose? She decided it wasn't.

'Sixteen is an awful age,' she thought. 'Really awful.'

Linda was shy and embarrassed about her appearance all the time. It hadn't been so bad at school, but now nobody seemed to know what she was going to do next. Her father talked about sending her to Paris next winter. Linda didn't want to go to Paris, but she didn't want to be at home, either. She hadn't realised until now how much she disliked Arlena.

'She's horrible,' she thought, '*horrible …*' Arlena wasn't unkind to her – most of the time she didn't even notice her – but she made her feel uncomfortable. There was something else too. What was it? 'She's bad,' Linda decided. 'She's really, truly bad.' Arlena did something to people. Her father had changed since meeting her. 'It'll continue like this – day after day, month after month. I can't stand it. I'd like to kill her. Oh, why doesn't she die?'

Linda remembered arriving at the hotel. It had been high tide, so they had arrived in a boat. The hotel had looked exciting and unusual. And then a tall, dark woman had called out her father's name.

He had called back: 'Rosamund! What a surprise!'

Linda liked Rosamund. She was sensible, she had nice hair, and she dressed nicely too. She had a friendly face and she had been pleasant to Linda. Her father had seemed pleased to see her too. He had looked suddenly different – younger – and he had laughed. That, Linda realised, was quite unusual.

'I wonder what father was like when he was my age,' she thought, but the idea was too difficult. Then she imagined, just for a moment, her father, Rosamund and herself – they could have such fun together on the island.

The blackness returned. Arlena. She couldn't be happy when there was someone there who she hated. Yes, hated. She hated Arlena.

◆

Kenneth Marshall knocked on his wife's bedroom door and went in. Arlena, dressed in green, was finishing her make-up in front of a mirror.

'Oh, it's you, Ken.'

Kenneth Marshall went to the window and looked out. 'You've met Patrick Redfern before, haven't you?' he said calmly.

'Yes, I have, at a party. I thought he was sweet.'

'Yes, that's clear. Did you know that he and his wife were coming here?'

'Oh no, that was the *greatest* surprise!'

'I thought, perhaps, that was why you wanted to come here so much.'

Arlena put down her make-up, turned and smiled at him.

'The Rylands told me that this place was wonderful. Don't you like it?'

'I'm not sure,' replied Marshall. 'But I can see that you plan to enjoy yourself. I suppose that you told young Redfern that you were coming here?'

'Oh dear, you aren't going to be horrible, are you?'

'Arlena,' said Kenneth, 'I know what you're like. They're a nice young couple. That young man is fond of his wife, really. Must you upset them?'

'That's so unfair,' replied Arlena. 'Don't blame me. I haven't done anything. It's not my fault if people go crazy about me. I don't do anything.'

'So you agree that young Redfern is crazy about you?'

'It's rather stupid of him,' Arlena moved towards her husband and looked up at him with wide eyes, 'but you know, Ken, I don't really care for anyone except you.'

'I think I know you quite well, Arlena,' he replied.

◆

From the hotel, there was a path that went round the cliff on the south-west side of the island. A little way along it, some steps led down to an area cut out of the cliff. This was known as Sunny **Ledge**, and there were some small specially-cut **caves** with seats in them. Patrick Redfern and his wife went to one of these immediately after dinner. They were silent for some time, and then Christine

---

ledge /ledʒ/ (n) a narrow shelf on the side of a cliff or mountain
cave /keɪv/ n a large hole (usually formed naturally) in the side of a mountain or rock

spoke in her quiet voice.

'Did you know that woman was going to be here?'

'I don't know what you mean.'

'Oh, Patrick! You really wanted to come here. I wanted to go to Tintagel again, but you made me come here because *she* was going to be here.'

'She? Who is *she*?'

'Mrs Marshall. You … you're in love with her.'

'Christine, don't be a fool. Married people are allowed to be friends with other people. Don't start getting jealous every time I speak to a pretty woman.'

'She isn't just a pretty woman. She's … she's different! She's bad. She'll hurt you, Patrick. Please, let's go away from here.'

'Don't be silly, Christine. And let's not argue about it. Let's go back.'

In the next little cave, Hercule Poirot sat and shook his head sadly. Some people might think that you should not listen to private conversations. But not Poirot.

Much later, he gave his explanation to his friend Hastings:

'It was all about murder.'

'But the murder hadn't happened then,' Hastings replied.

'No, but there were already clear signs, my friend.'

'Then why didn't you stop it?'

And Hercule Poirot replied sadly that if somebody is planning a murder, it is not easy to stop them. He didn't blame himself for what happened. It had to happen.

2.1 Were you right?

Look back at your answers to Activity 1.2 on page iv and correct the sentences that are wrong. Then write the correct names below.

Who ...

1 thinks that bodies are like meat? ....

2 sees a ghost? ....

3 likes boats? ....

4 doesn't want to burn in the sun? ....

5 talks about madness? ....

6 lies down by a rock? ....

7 has lived in India? ....

8 sells clothes? ....

9 wants to kill someone? ....

10 listens to a private conversation? ....

2.2 What more did you learn?

1 Look at the picture on page 3. Discuss who each character is and what you know about them.

2 Complete the sentences about these characters.

    a Mr and Mrs Gardener are from ....

    b Arlena Marshall used to be called ....

    c Stephen Lane thinks .... is everywhere.

    d Rosamund Darnley used to know ....

    e ....'s mother was suspected of murder.

    f Christine Redfern used to be a ....

    g .... and .... don't like heights.

    h .... is crazy about Arlena.

2.3 Language in use

Read the sentences in the box.
Then complete the sentences
below with second conditional
verb forms.

'That **would** soon **disappear**, Monsieur Poirot,
if you **took** a rowing-boat out each day.'

'**I'd be** happier **if I were** poor, with a husband
and children.'

1   You .... (soon get) fit if you ....

   .... (do) more exercise.

2   If I .... (be) rich, I ....

   (travel) round the world.

3   If you .... (can) choose a holiday, what kind of trip

   .... (you/choose)?

4   I .... (go) to the beach if I ....

   .... (not have) any school work.

5   .... (we/really be) happier if we ....

   .... (have) more money?

2.4 What happens next?

Look at the pictures in Chapters 3 and 4 and discuss the questions. What do
you think? Make notes in your notebook.

1   Page 14   Who are these people and what is their relationship?
         What are they talking about?

2   Page 18   Who has Poirot seen? What are they saying to each other?

3   Page 19   Why is Linda rowing away from the island?

4   Page 20   Who is Linda going to meet, and why is she anxious?

5   Page 21   What is Poirot doing? Where is Arlena going?

6   Page 24   Who are in the boat? What have they seen?
         What has just happened?

CHAPTER 3

That Poor Little Woman

'I think, Monsieur Redfern, that you enjoy life?
May I offer you some advice? Stay away from women.'

Rosamund Darnley and Kenneth Marshall sat on the grassy top of the cliff, looking out over Gull Cove. It was on the east side of the island, where people sometimes came in the morning for a peaceful swim.

'It's nice to get away from people,' said Rosamund.

'Mmmm, yes, it is,' replied Kenneth. 'Do you remember the hills at Shipley? Those were good days. You haven't changed much. You've been very successful and you're rich, but you're the same Rosamund.'

'I don't think so! Isn't it a pity that we can't always be the same nice people as when we were young?'

'I'm not sure that you were *ever* a nice person. You used to have a terrible temper. You nearly **strangled** me once!'

Rosamund laughed, then became serious. 'Ken, if I say something very rude, will you never speak to me again?'

Kenneth looked at her with surprise. 'I don't think I would ever think you were rude. You *belong*.'

Rosamund nodded, hiding her pleasure at his words. 'Kenneth, why don't you divorce your wife?'

His face changed. He took a pipe from his pocket and began filling it.

'I'm sorry if I've offended you.'

'You haven't offended me. But you don't understand. I married her.'

'I know. But there's a lot of talk about her. You *could* divorce her, Ken.'

'Men go crazy about her, but that doesn't mean she goes crazy about *them*.'

strangle /ˈstræŋgəl/ (v) to kill someone by pressing their throat tightly

'You could make *her* divorce *you*, if you prefer. You ought to, Ken. Really, I mean it. Arlena's not good for Linda. Linda *feels* things a lot.'

'Yes, that may be true. Arlena and Linda aren't very good for each other. Linda's like her mother. She's easily hurt.'

'Then don't you think you ought to divorce Arlena? People do it all the time.'

'Yes, they do,' said Kenneth Marshall angrily. 'But if you marry a woman and promise to look after her, you should do it. Arlena's my wife.'

Rosamund bent towards him. She said in a low voice, 'So you'll be with her, as you promised in church, until the two of you are separated by death?'

Kenneth Marshall nodded. 'Yes,' he said, 'that's it.'

◆

Mr Horace Blatt was driving along a narrow country road when he nearly hit Mrs Redfern. He stopped his car and said cheerfully, 'Hello, hello!'

He was a large man with a red face. It seemed to be Mr Blatt's desire to be loud and friendly wherever he went. He was surprised that people often disappeared when they saw him coming.

'I nearly hit you, didn't I?' he said happily. 'Jump in.'

'Oh, thanks, but I think I'll walk.'

'Rubbish,' said Mr Blatt. 'What's a car for?'

Christine got into the car and Mr Blatt started the engine.

'Why are you walking alone? That's wrong, a nice-looking girl like you.'

'Oh, I like being alone.'

'Girls always say that, but they don't mean it. You know, that hotel is too dull. There's no *life* there. There are a lot of dull guests. There's that boring old man who lived in India, and that strange reverend; those Americans who talk too much, and that foreigner with a moustache. That moustache makes me laugh! I'd guess he's a hairdresser.'

'No,' said Christine, 'he's a detective.' Mr Blatt nearly drove off the road. 'He's Hercule Poirot. Surely you've heard of him?'

'Oh yes,' said Mr Blatt. 'I thought he was dead. What's he doing here?'

'He isn't doing anything. He's on holiday.'

'Well, I suppose that might be true … I don't like him, do you?'

'Well,' said Christine, 'perhaps he is a little strange.'

Mr Blatt reached the bottom of the hill and drove into the hotel's garage, which was on the mainland.

◆

Linda Marshall was also on the mainland, in a small shop which lent books to its customers for two pence each. She looked at one or two, and then she noticed a small book with a brown leather cover. Time passed …

Linda put the book quickly back on the shelf as Christine Redfern's voice said, 'What are you reading, Linda?'

'Nothing,' said Linda quickly. 'I'm looking for a book.'

'Mr Blatt just drove me here – after he'd nearly knocked me down first. I didn't want to walk to the hotel with him, so I said I had to buy some things.'

'He's awful, isn't he?' said Linda. 'He always says how rich he is and he makes the most terrible jokes.'

'Poor man,' said Christine. 'One feels rather sorry for him.'

Linda didn't. She walked with Christine out of the shop and down towards the hotel. She was busy with her own thoughts. Christine Redfern and Rosamund Darnley were the only people on the island who she liked. Neither of them talked much.

'Mrs Redfern,' Linda said suddenly, 'have you ever felt that everything's really awful – really terrible?'

'Yes,' said Christine, looking at Linda's anxious face, 'I have.'

◆

'So,' said Mr Blatt, 'you're the famous detective?'

He was sitting with Hercule Poirot in the hotel bar, which was one of Mr Blatt's favourite places. Poirot nodded.

'And what are you doing here – are you working?'

'No, no, I am resting. I am on holiday.'

Mr Blatt smiled. 'You have to say that! You can talk openly to me. I don't repeat what I hear! I learnt to keep quiet years ago. But most people talk, talk, talk about everything! You can't have that in your job! That's why you have to pretend you're here on holiday.'

'But why do you suppose that I am pretending?' asked Poirot.

'I know people. A man like you would take a holiday in France! I've had to work hard all my life. Now I'm successful and I can do what I want.'

'I, too, wondered. I would certainly expect you to take a holiday in France!'

Mr Blatt laughed. 'And we're both here, instead! I think it sounded romantic. Smugglers' Island! I used to sail when I was a boy, and I've always loved it. I like spending time in my little boat. Redfern likes sailing too. He's been out with me a few times, but now he's always chasing that red-haired woman, Mrs Marshall.' He paused and then continued, in a lower voice, 'I imagine that Marshall has problems with her! Men go crazy about her. There'll be trouble one of these days. I guess Marshall's a man with a temper. I've met that quiet sort. You never know what they'll do. Redfern had better be careful …'

He stopped as Patrick Redfern came into the bar. Then he continued, loudly. 'And, as I was saying, sailing is good fun. Hello, Redfern! Have a drink!'

'Sailing?' said Patrick Redfern, as he sat down. 'It's the best fun in the world. I used to sail round this coast when I was a boy.'

'Then you know this area well?' said Poirot.

'Oh yes,' replied Redfern. 'I knew it before there was a hotel here. There used to be an old house. There were lots of stories of a secret way to get from the house to Pixy Cave. We were always looking for it.'

Horace Blatt dropped his glass and his drink went everywhere. 'What is this Pixy Cave?' he asked.

'It's in Pixy *Cove*,' said Redfern. 'You have to squeeze through some big rocks, then there's quite a big natural cave. It was great fun when I was a boy! These days, nobody seems to know about it.'

'I'm going in to dinner,' said Horace Blatt.

◆

'Do you know Monsieur Blatt well?' Poirot asked Redfern when the large man had left.

'Not really. I've only been sailing with him once or twice. He prefers being alone.'

'That is strange,' said Poirot. 'He is not like that on land.'

'I know. It's difficult to keep out of his way!' Redfern laughed.

Poirot was studying Redfern's face. Suddenly, he said, 'I think, Monsieur Redfern, that you enjoy life? May I offer you some advice? Stay away from women.'

'I'm afraid it's a bit late for that. I'm married.'

'I know. Your wife is lovely. She is, I think, very fond of you.'

'I'm very fond of *her*,' replied Patrick Redfern. 'What are you trying to say, Poirot?'

'*Les femmes*.*' Poirot sat back and closed his eyes. 'They can make life complicated. If you had to come here, why did you bring your wife?'

'I don't know what you mean,' said Redfern angrily. 'You've been listening to the other guests. She's good-looking, so they're horrible about her.'

'Are you really so young?' said Poirot quietly as he left the bar. Patrick Redfern stared angrily after him.

◆

Poirot stepped outside. It was a fine night. He found Mrs Redfern in her favourite seat on the cliff.

'You shouldn't sit here,' he said. 'You will catch a cold.'

'No, I won't. And it doesn't matter if I do.'

'It has been raining, and there were clouds, but now the sky is clear and there are stars above. That is like life, Madame.'

'I hate pity. Everybody says, "poor little Mrs Redfern". I hate it!'

* *les femmes*: French for *women*

17

'Let me tell you something that is as true as the stars,' said Poirot. 'The Arlenas of this world do not matter. To be truly important, a woman must have goodness or brains. Your husband loves you, Madame, I know it.'

She started crying on Poirot's shoulder.

'Be patient – just be patient,' Poirot said softly.

'I'm better now.' Christine sat up. 'Leave me. I'd like to be alone.'

Poirot obeyed, and followed the path back down to the hotel. He was nearly there when he heard voices. He heard Patrick's voice, full of emotion.

'I'm crazy about you – crazy. Do you care a little – do you care?'

He saw Arlena's face – the face of a happy cat. Animal, not human.

'Of course, Patrick. I love you. You know that …'

Unusually, Hercule Poirot did not stay to listen. He was soon joined on the path by Kenneth Marshall.

'It's a fine night, isn't it?' said Marshall, looking up at the sky. 'We'll have good weather tomorrow.'

CHAPTER 4

A Terrible Discovery

Emily Brewster heard his voice – a small, frightened whisper.
'My God, she's dead …'

August 25th was a bright, sunny day, and several people at the Jolly Roger Hotel got up early. At eight o'clock, Linda was looking at a little book with a brown leather cover. Her lips were tightly closed, and her eyes narrowed.

'I'll do it …' she whispered to herself.

She put on her swimsuit, with a summer dress over it, left her room and went out onto a first floor **balcony**. As she was going down the steps from the balcony to the beach, she met her father coming up.

'You're up early. Are you going for a swim?'

Linda nodded, but instead of going to the beach, she went round the hotel until she was opposite the mainland. The tide was high, but the little boat was there. Linda got in, untied it, and rowed herself across.

The woman had just opened the shop and was busy sweeping the floor.

'Well, Miss, you *are* up early,' she said.

Linda put her hand in the pocket of her dress and took out some money.

◆

Christine Redfern was standing in Linda's room when the girl returned.

balcony /ˈbælkəni/ (n) a small area outside an upstairs window where you can sit or stand

19

'Oh, there you are!' she said. 'I thought you couldn't be up so early.'

'I've been for a swim.'

Noticing the package in Linda's hand, Christine added, 'The post is early today!'

Linda looked embarrassed. She dropped the package and some things fell out.

'Why have you been buying **candles**?' asked Christine, as she helped to pick the things up. Without waiting for a reply, she continued, 'I came to ask if you'd like to come with me to Gull Cove this morning. I want to do some drawing.'

Linda accepted with pleasure. In the last few days she had gone on several drawing trips with Christine. Linda liked being with Christine, who didn't speak much when she was busy with her work. She and Christine seemed to understand each other, probably because they both disliked the same person.

'I'm playing tennis at twelve,' said Christine, 'so we'd better start quite early. Half past ten?'

'Right. I'll be ready. I'll meet you in the hall.'

◆

Rosamund Darnley was walking out of the dining-room after a very late breakfast when Linda ran down the stairs and crashed into her.

'Oh! Sorry, Miss Darnley. I'm going with Mrs Redfern to Gull Cove. I said I'd meet her at half past ten. I thought I was late.'

'No, it's only twenty-five past.' Rosamund looked at Linda's hot face. 'You aren't ill, are you, Linda?'

candle /ˈkændl/ (n) a white or coloured stick that you burn to produce light

20

'Oh no, I'm never ill.'

Rosamund smiled. 'It's such a lovely day,' she said, 'that I got up for breakfast. I usually have it in bed, but today I came downstairs.'

'I know. It's beautiful. I shall put a lot of suntan oil on and get really brown.'

'Yes, Gull Cove is nice in the morning, and more peaceful than the beach.'

'Come with us,' said Linda, rather shyly.

But Rosamund shook her head. 'Not this morning. I have something else to do.'

Christine Redfern came down the stairs. She was wearing long, loose trousers and a matching blouse. They were made of a green and yellow material. Rosamund wanted to tell her that yellow and green were the worst colours for someone with her pale skin.

She thought, 'If I chose that girl's clothes, I'd soon make her husband notice her. Arlena's a fool, but she certainly knows what to wear.'

'Have a nice time,' she said. 'I'm going to Sunny Ledge with a book.'

◆

Hercule Poirot had breakfast in his room, but it was such a beautiful morning that he went down to the beach at ten o'clock, half an hour earlier than usual. The beach was empty except for one person – Arlena Marshall.

She was wearing her white swimsuit and the green Chinese hat, and she was getting into a little white boat. Poirot, always a gentleman, went to help, and got his white leather shoes very wet.

As she was rowing away, Arlena called, 'Monsieur Poirot, will you do something for me? Don't tell anyone where I am.' She smiled sweetly. 'I just want to be *alone*, for a change.'

'*Jamais**!' said Poirot quietly to himself. 'I do not believe that!'

Hercule Poirot, the man of the world, knew better. She was going to meet someone, and he thought he knew who. But then he discovered he was wrong.

Just as Arlena's boat went out of sight, Patrick Redfern came down from the hotel, followed by Kenneth Marshall.

'Morning, Poirot,' said Marshall. 'Have you seen my wife anywhere?'

'Has she got up so early?' replied Poirot, carefully.

'She's not in her room,' said Marshall. 'It's a lovely day. I'll go swimming right now.'

Patrick Redfern was looking up and down the beach. He sat down near Poirot and prepared to wait for his lady.

'And Madame Redfern? Has she got up early too?'

'She's going to do some drawing. She's enjoying her art at the moment.'

He was clearly thinking about something else. At every footstep he turned to see who was coming down from the hotel. Each time, it was the wrong person. First, Mr and Mrs Gardener arrived. Then Miss Brewster. Mrs Gardener sat down and began to knit and talk.

'Well, Monsieur Poirot, the beach seems empty. Where is everybody?'

Marshall had just finished his swim, and came up to them. 'It's great in the sea,' he said. 'Unfortunately I've got a lot of work to do. I must go and do it.'

'That's a pity, on a beautiful day like this,' Mrs Gardener said. 'Wasn't yesterday terrible? I said to Mr Gardener that if the weather stayed bad we'd have to leave. And where's your daughter this morning, Mr Marshall? You know, that girl looks pale. She needs some good food and kindness.'

'Linda's all right,' said Kenneth Marshall coldly, and he went up to the hotel.

Patrick Redfern started walking up and down the beach, staring up at the hotel and looking annoyed. Mrs Gardener continued to talk.

'I was saying this morning,' she said, 'that we really must go on a trip to Dartmoor†. It's quite close and it sounds so romantic. And I'd like to see the prison there. I think we should arrange it for tomorrow, Odell.'

'Are you going to swim, Mademoiselle?' Poirot asked Miss Brewster.

'Oh no, I had my morning swim before breakfast. Somebody hit me on the head with a bottle on my way back – threw it out of one of the hotel windows.'

'That's very dangerous!' said Mrs Gardener. 'I had a dear friend who was hit

---

* *jamais*: French for *never*

† Dartmoor: a large area of open countryside in south-west England

by a tin of toothpaste which was thrown out of a thirty-fifth floor window.' She began to look through her wool. 'Odell, I haven't got that purple wool. It's in the drawer in our room.'

'Yes, dear,' Mr Gardener stood up and went on his search.

Poirot looked down sadly at his white shoes.

'Have you been in the sea in your shoes?' asked Emily Brewster.

'Oh dear, yes,' said Poirot. 'I was too much in a hurry.'

'Where's the big star this morning?' asked Miss Brewster, softly. 'She's late.'

Mrs Gardener looked up from her knitting and watched Patrick Redfern.

'He looks angry,' she said. 'Just like a wild animal. Oh dear, I wonder what Mr Marshall thinks about it all. He's such a nice quiet man. You never know what he's thinking.'

Three pairs of eyes watched Patrick Redfern. He looked very angry now. In the distance they could hear a faint sound from the mainland.

'The wind's in the east again,' said Emily Brewster. 'It's a good sign when you can hear the church clock.'

Nobody spoke again until Mr Gardener returned with the wool.

'What a long time you've been, Odell!'

'Sorry, dear, it wasn't where you said. I found it in the cupboard.'

'Well, how strange! I was sure it was in the drawer! Luckily, I've never been a witness in court. I'd worry about it so much!'

'Are you going rowing this morning, Miss Brewster?' asked Patrick Redfern, five minutes later. 'Do you mind if I come with you?'

'No, that's fine,' replied Miss Brewster cheerfully.

'Let's row right round the island,' Patrick said.

Miss Brewster looked at her watch. 'Will we have time? Yes, it isn't half past eleven yet. Let's start.'

◆

Patrick Redfern rowed first. He rowed powerfully, and the boat moved fast.

'Good,' said Miss Brewster. 'We'll see if you can continue like this.'

'My hands will probably hurt by the time we get back,' he laughed.

They moved out to sea and rowed under the cliffs. Patrick looked up.

'Is anyone on Sunny Ledge this morning? Yes, who's that?'

'It's Miss Darnley, I think.'

They rowed up the coast. On their left was the open sea. Patrick was still rowing hard, and at the same time he was looking carefully at the cliffs.

'He's looking for that Marshall woman!' thought Emily Brewster suddenly. 'That's why he wanted to come with me.'

They went round a rock to the south of Pixy Cove. It was a small cove, with a beach and some rocks. The cliff hung over it. In the morning, with no sun on it, there was rarely anyone there, but this time there was someone on the beach.

'Who's that?' asked Patrick Redfern.

'It looks like Mrs Marshall.'

Patrick Redfern started rowing towards the beach.

'Poor boy,' Miss Brewster thought. 'He really is crazy about her. Oh well, never mind.'

The boat was getting closer to the shore fast. Miss Brewster could see Arlena more clearly now, lying face down on the beach, with her arms stretched out. The white boat was near her.

Emily Brewster suddenly felt that something was wrong. Arlena had often lain like this on the beach near the hotel, her tanned body stretched out face down in the sun, the green cardboard hat protecting her head and neck. But there was no sun on Pixy beach.

The boat landed and Patrick called out, 'Hello, Arlena.'

And then Emily Brewster became really worried; the figure did not move or answer.

Emily saw Patrick's face change. He jumped out of the boat and she followed him. They ran up the beach to the figure, which still had not moved. Patrick Redfern got there first but Emily Brewster was close behind him. She saw, as one sees in a dream, the brown arms and legs, the white swimsuit, red hair showing from under the green hat. The body was lying in a strange, unnatural way. She felt, then, that this body had not *lain* down – it had been *thrown* down... .

Patrick Redfern bent down and touched the hand. Emily Brewster heard his voice – a small, frightened whisper.

'*My God, she's dead ...*'

And then, as he lifted the hat and looked at the back of the neck, '*Oh, God, she's been strangled ... murdered.*'

Time stopped for Emily Brewster. She heard herself saying, 'We mustn't touch anything until the police come.'

'No, no, of course not.' Redfern spoke like a machine. Then he whispered, 'Who? *Who?* Who could do that to Arlena? It can't be true.'

Emily Brewster shook her head. She heard the anger in his voice as he continued, 'My God, if I get my hands on the evil person who did this, I'll ...'

'Whoever did this wouldn't stay here,' she said. 'We must call the police. Perhaps ...' she paused, 'one of us ought to stay with ... with the body.'

'I'll stay,' said Patrick Redfern.

Emily Brewster was secretly grateful. She didn't want to stay alone on that beach with the faint possibility of a mad murderer close by.

'Good,' she said. 'I'll be as quick as I can. I'll go in the boat. I don't want to go up the cliff on the ladder. There's a police station on the mainland.'

As she rowed fast away from the shore, Emily Brewster watched Patrick Redfern. He dropped down beside the dead woman and put his head in his hands. He looked like a dog watching his dead owner.

Then she said to herself, 'It's the best thing that could happen, for him and his wife, and for Marshall and the child – but I don't suppose he can see it like that, poor man.'

3.1 Were you right?

Look back at your answers to Activity 2.4. Then match the beginnings of the sentences with the correct endings. Write the letters a–f.

1 Rosamund Darnley and Kenneth Marshall are ... .

2 Arlena and Patrick are ... .

3 Linda is ... .

4 In the next picture, she is ... .

5 Arlena is ... .

6 Patrick Redfern and Miss Brewster are ... .

    a saying that they love each other.

    b hurrying to meet Christine.

    c talking about childhood memories.

    d looking at a body on the beach.

    e going to the shop on the mainland.

    f saying that she wants to be alone.

3.2 What more did you learn?

Circle the correct names.

1 Kenneth Marshall remembers *Rosamund Darnley's / Arlena Marshall's* bad temper.

2 Horace Blatt thinks that *Kenneth Marshall / Patrick Redfern* has a bad temper.

3 Poirot thinks that *Arlena Marshall / Christine Redfern* is very fond of Patrick.

4 *Linda Marshall / Christine Redfern* buys candles on the mainland.

5 Poirot doesn't believe that *Christine Redfern / Arlena Marshall* ever wants to be alone.

6 *Emily Brewster / Linda Marshall* was hit by a bottle that was thrown out of a hotel window.

7 *Mr Gardener / Mrs Gardener* finds purple wool in the wrong place.

8 *Patrick Redfern / Emily Brewster* suggests a trip round the island.

9 *Emily Brewster / Patrick Redfern* goes to fetch the police.

3.3 **Language in use**

Read the sentences in the box. Then match the sentences below and complete the advice. Write one word in each space.

> 'Redfern **had better be** careful.'
>
> 'I think we **should arrange** it for tomorrow, Odell.'
>
> 'Perhaps one of us **ought to stay** with the body.'

1   The sun is very hot.   ...c...
2   I haven't sent any postcards yet.   ....
3   The tide is quite strong.   ....
4   They're having a conversation.   ....
5   This road is very narrow.   ....
6   It's very late.   ....

a   Swimmers .... be careful.
b   You .... drive too fast.
c   You .... *ought* .... to wear a hat.
d   I ought .... go to bed.
e   I'd .... write some now.
f   We .... better
    .... interrupt them.

3.4 **What happens next?**

1   The pictures show the first guests that Poirot and the police interview. Who is each question for, do you think?

a   What time did you go to Linda's room?
    ....

b   Where did you usually meet Arlena?
    ....

c   When did you last see your wife?
    ....

d   Was your family happy?
    ....

2   What other questions will they ask, do you think? Discuss your ideas.

CHAPTER 5

Interviews and Alibis

*'Nine times out of ten, murder results from the
character and situation of the murdered person.'*

Inspector Colgate stood by the cliff, waiting for the doctor to finish with
Arlena's body. Patrick Redfern and Emily Brewster stood near him.

'She's been strangled,' said Dr Neasden, 'by quite a powerful pair of hands.'

'What about the time of death?' asked Inspector Colgate.

'Let's see … It's quarter to one now. What time did you find her?'

'Some time before twelve. I don't know exactly,' said Patrick Redfern.

'It was quarter to twelve when we found she was dead,' said Miss Brewster.

'Ah, and you came here by boat. What time was it when you noticed her?'

'About five or six minutes earlier.' She turned to Redfern. 'Do you agree?'

'Yes, yes, about that, I think,' said Redfern absently.

'Is this the husband?' Neasden asked the Inspector in a low voice. 'Oh! I see.
My mistake. I thought it might be. He seems rather upset.'

'Let's say it happened at twenty minutes to twelve,' he said, more loudly. 'I'd
say between eleven and eleven forty – quarter to eleven at the earliest.'

'Thanks.' The inspector shut his notebook. 'Less than an hour. That will help
a lot. Now, I think we'll go to the hotel.'

Inspector /ɪnˈspektə/ (n) a British police officer

'Well, this is a surprise, seeing you again!' said **Chief Constable** Weston. 'Here you are at the scene of another murder. Are you going to help us? I don't know yet whether it's a problem for Scotland Yard*. Our murderer is probably quite close. But all these people are strangers here. We'll have to go to London to find out about them and their **motives**.'

Poirot nodded, as Weston continued. 'First, we have to find out who last saw the dead woman alive. A servant took her breakfast to her at nine. A girl in the office saw her pass through the sitting-room and then go out at about ten.'

'My friend,' said Poirot, 'I suspect that I am the man you want. I saw her at five minutes past ten. I helped her with her boat, at the beach. She went round there, to the right. Towards Pixy Cove. I believe she actually left the beach at a quarter past ten.'

'That fits,' said Weston. 'How long would it take to get round to the cove?'

'Ah, I do not go in boats. Perhaps half an hour?'

'That's about what I think,' said Weston. 'She wasn't hurrying, I imagine. Well, if she arrived there at quarter to eleven, that fits well enough.'

'What time does your doctor think she died?'

'Neasden didn't say exactly. A quarter to eleven at the earliest.'

'There is one other thing,' said Poirot. 'Mrs Marshall asked me not to say I had seen her.'

Weston stared. 'Hmm,' he said. 'That's interesting. Listen, Poirot, you're a man of the world. What sort of woman was she? I know what the women say, but is it true? *Was* she having a relationship with this man Redfern?'

'I would say undoubtedly *yes*. And it seems that he followed her here.'

'And the husband – did he know about it? What did he feel?'

'It is not easy to know what Mr Marshall feels or thinks. He does not show his emotions.'

'But he might *have* feelings.'

'Oh yes,' said Poirot, 'He might.'

◆

The chief constable was choosing his words carefully with Mrs Castle, the owner of the Jolly Roger Hotel.

'I can't believe something like this has happened in my hotel! My guests are such nice people! No loud behaviour. Not like the big hotels in St Loo.'

'Accidents happen, Mrs Castle. We're not blaming you in any way.'

'But it's so bad for my hotel,' she cried. 'Of course, only hotel guests are allowed

* Scotland Yard: the department of British police that deals with serious national crime

Chief Constable /ˌtʃiːf ˈkʌnstəbəl/ (n) the police officer in charge of the police in a large area of Britain. A *constable* is a low-level police officer.

motive /ˈməʊtɪv/ (n) the reason why someone does something, especially something bad

on to the island, but I expect people will still *point* from the shore.'

'Yes, how do you keep the holiday crowds off the island?'

'Well, of course at high tide we're separated from the mainland.'

'Yes, but what about at low tide?'

She explained that at the end of the island nearest the mainland there was a gate, with a notice saying, 'Jolly Roger Hotel. Private.' There were rocks on both sides, which were too high to climb.

'But you couldn't stop someone rowing round to one of the coves?'

This, it seemed, rarely happened. It was a long way to row, and hard work. There were notices, too, on Gull Cove and Pixy Cove, and George and William always watched the beach that was nearest the mainland.

'Who are George and William?'

'They work for me. George looks after the beach and William is the gardener.'

'Well, that seems clear enough,' said Weston impatiently. 'It's possible that someone came from outside, but if they did, they knew they might be noticed. Now, Mrs Castle, can I see a list of the hotel guests?'

He studied the book, and looked over to Poirot. 'You'll be able to help us with this in a moment. What about the servants, Mrs Castle?'

'There are four servants and four waiters, and Henry in the bar. William cleans the boots and shoes. Then there are three cooks. All nice young people.'

'Thank you, Mrs Castle,' said Weston. 'Now I must talk to Mr Marshall.'

◆

Kenneth Marshall's face was serious but he was quite calm.

'This must be a terrible shock for you,' Weston said, 'but you realise that I'm anxious to get all the information quickly.' Marshall nodded. 'Mrs Marshall was your wife?'

'Yes, we've been married just over four years.'

'And her name before she was married?'

'Helen Stuart. Her acting name was Arlena Stuart.'

'Did she give up acting when she married?'

'No. She only stopped about a year and a half ago, when she was tired of it.'

'You didn't ... tell her to stop? You didn't argue about it?'

'No,' said Marshall. 'My wife was free to please herself.'

'And – the marriage was a happy one?'

'Certainly,' said Kenneth Marshall, coldly.

'Have you any idea who killed your wife? Did she have any enemies?'

'Possibly. My wife was an actress. She was also very good-looking. Both these things made people jealous. There were arguments with other actresses, but that doesn't mean that any of them was a murderer.'

'What you really mean, Monsieur,' said Poirot, 'is that her enemies were *women*?'

'Yes,' said Kenneth Marshall. 'That's right.'

'Had she met any of the guests in this hotel before you came here?'

'I believe she had met Mr Redfern before. I don't think anybody else.'

'When was the last time you saw your wife this morning?' Weston asked.

'I looked into her room on my way to breakfast, at about nine o'clock. She was opening her letters.'

'How did she seem? Was she excited, or sad, or upset in any way?'

'I certainly didn't notice anything.'

'Did she say what her letters contained?'

'I think she said they were bills,' said Marshall, with a faint smile on his lips.

'Your wife had breakfast in bed?'

'Yes, she always did that. She usually came downstairs between ten and eleven – usually nearer eleven.'

'But this morning she came down at exactly ten o'clock. Is that surprising?'

'Yes. Perhaps it was the weather – an extra fine day, you know. I was surprised that her room was empty after breakfast.'

'And then you came down on the beach and asked me if I had seen her?'

'Er, yes. And you said you hadn't …'

Hercule Poirot's innocent eyes looked straight at Marshall.

'How well did your wife know Mr Redfern?' asked Weston, in a lower voice.

'Do you mind if I smoke?' said Kenneth Marshall, 'Oh! I've left my pipe somewhere.' Poirot offered him a cigarette, which he accepted. 'You were asking about Redfern. My wife told me she had met him at a party.'

'Since then,' Weston paused, 'I understand that they have become rather closer friends. Everyone at the hotel is talking about it.'

For a moment, Marshall looked at Poirot with cold anger in his eyes.

'Stories like that are usually quite untrue.'

'Possibly, but Mr Redfern and your wife were always together. You did not – excuse me, Mr Marshall – mind that?'

'I never criticised my wife. And I don't listen to stupid stories.'

'And if we have a witness who says they were lovers?'

Marshall's blue eyes looked coldly at Poirot again. 'My wife's dead and she can't defend herself. I think you're forgetting what's important – the plain fact of murder.'

'You do not understand, my friend,' said Poirot. 'There is no plain murder. Nine times out of ten, murder results from the character and situation of the murdered person. Until we understand *exactly what kind of person Arlena was,* we won't know exactly *the kind of person who murdered her*. And you can

congratulate yourself – you have done nothing to help me!'

'You're crazy,' said Marshall, and he looked towards the chief constable. 'Is there anything else that *you'd* like to ask me?'

'Yes, Mr Marshall. Please tell me everything you did this morning.'

'I had breakfast downstairs at nine o'clock. I went up to my wife's room afterwards and found that she had gone out. I came down to the beach and asked Monsieur Poirot if he had seen her. Then I had a quick swim and went up to the hotel at about twenty to eleven. I went to my room, but the girl hadn't finished cleaning it, so I asked her to finish quickly. I had some letters to type which I wanted to post. I went downstairs and spoke to Henry in the bar. I went up again to my room at ten to eleven and typed my letters until ten to twelve. I then changed into my tennis clothes because I had arranged to play tennis at twelve. We'd booked the court the day before.'

'Who do you mean by "we"?'

'Mrs Redfern, Miss Darnley, Mr Gardener and I. I came down at twelve and went to the court. Miss Darnley was there with Mr Gardener. Mrs Redfern arrived a few minutes later. We played tennis for an hour. As we came into the hotel afterwards, I – I – got the news.'

'Thank you, Mr Marshall. I have to ask – did anyone see you when you were typing in your room between – er – ten to eleven and ten to twelve?'

'Have you got an idea that I killed my wife?' said Kenneth Marshall with a faint smile. 'The servant was somewhere near. I'm sure she heard the typewriter. And I haven't posted the letters. I imagine they are **evidence**.' He took three letters from his pocket. 'They contain private financial information. If you tell one of your men to copy them, he won't do it in less than an hour.'

'One more thing,' said Weston. 'Do you know who your wife has left her money to?'

'I don't think there's a legal document, so her money will come to me.'

'But she probably had little to leave?'

'You're quite wrong. Only two years ago, Sir Roger Erskine, an old friend of hers, died and left her most of his money. About fifty thousand pounds.'

Inspector Colgate looked up and spoke for the first time. 'Then your wife was a rich woman? And she didn't leave any instructions?'

'You can check. But I'm sure she didn't. Do you want anything else?'

'No,' said Weston. 'Mr Marshall, I'm very sorry about your wife's death.'

◆

'We must ask ourselves about motive,' said Colgate. 'Her husband is the only person who will make money from her death. But what about jealousy? Her husband didn't agree that she had any real enemies, but I don't believe that can be true.'

'Yes,' said Poirot, 'I am sure Arlena Marshall made enemies. But, Inspector, Arlena's enemies were, I think, always women. It does not seem possible that the murderer was a woman. What is the medical evidence?'

'Neasden's confident that she was strangled by a man. Big, powerful hands. It's possible that a very strong woman did it, but it's very unlikely.'

'Exactly,' said Poirot, nodding. 'Poison, a knife, even a gun – but strangling – no! We have to look for a man. There are two people here in this hotel who have a motive, and both of them are women.'

'Redfern's wife is one of them, I suppose?' asked Weston.

'Yes. It's possible that Mrs Redfern decided to kill Arlena. She had a good reason. But she is not, in my opinion, a woman of strong emotions. I am also sure that she could not strangle someone – her hands are small.'

'I have an idea,' said Colgate. 'Imagine that before she met Mr Redfern, the lady had a relationship with someone – let's call him X. She leaves X for Mr Redfern. Mad with anger and jealousy, X follows her here and kills her.'

'Yes, it's possible,' said Weston. 'And it ought to be easy to prove. Did he come on foot or did he hire a boat? What do you think, Poirot?'

Poirot shook his head and said, 'Somewhere, there is something that we have missed.'

evidence /ˈevɪdəns/ (n) information or things that make you believe something is true

CHAPTER 6

Evidence and Ideas

*'When Redfern arrived at the beach, he was very clearly looking for her!
Therefore, I ask myself, who was Arlena Marshall going to meet?'*

Weston, Colgate and Poirot were studying the list of guests at the hotel.
'The Gardeners are a pleasant, middle-aged married couple, who have
travelled a lot,' said Poirot. 'The lady does all the talking; the husband just agrees
with her. He plays tennis and has a nice sense of humour. Next – the Redferns.
Mr Redfern is young and attractive, an excellent swimmer, a good tennis
player and a good dancer. His wife is quiet and pretty, and I think she loves her
husband. She has something that Arlena Marshall did not have – brains.'

'Brains aren't very useful in matters of love,' said Inspector Colgate.

'Perhaps not. But I really believe that although he was crazy about Mrs
Marshall, Patrick Redfern cares for his wife.'

'That may be true. It wouldn't be the first time.'

'Major Barry,' Poirot continued, 'used to be in the Indian army. He admires
women. He tells long and boring stories. Mr Horace Blatt is, it seems, a rich
businessman. He wants to be everybody's friend, but nobody likes him much.
He asked me a lot of questions last night. He was worried. Yes, there is

something not quite right about Mr Blatt. Next, Miss Rosamund Darnley. She has a fashion business and is also known as Rose Mond. She has brains, she is attractive.' He paused, then added, 'And she is an old friend of Mr Marshall.'

'Oh, is she?' Weston sat up in his chair.

'Yes. They had not met for some years. She says that she did not know he would be here.' Poirot paused again. 'Miss Brewster. I am a little afraid of her. She has a voice like a man's. She is very fit and strong. She rows boats and is good at tennis. But I think she has a good heart.'

'That leaves only Reverend Stephen Lane,' said Weston. 'Who's he?'

'I can only tell you that he is a very nervous and excitable man.'

'And that's all of them!' said Weston. 'But you are thoughtful, my friend.'

'Yes,' said Poirot. 'When Mrs Marshall went out this morning, I thought that she was going to meet Redfern somewhere and that she did not want her husband to know ... but I was wrong. When Redfern arrived at the beach, he was very clearly looking for her! Therefore, I ask myself, *who was Arlena Marshall going to meet?*'

'Well,' said Weston, 'we can think about that later. We have to get through these interviews. We'd better see the Marshall girl next.'

Linda came into the room a little too quickly. She was breathing fast and looked like a frightened young animal.

'Poor child,' thought Weston. 'There's nothing to worry about,' he said kindly. 'We just want you to tell us anything that might be useful.'

'Do you mean – about Arlena?'

'Yes. Did you see her this morning?'

'No. Arlena always comes down rather late. She has breakfast in bed.'

'Will you tell us what you did this morning?'

'I had a swim, then breakfast. Then I went with Mrs Redfern to Gull Cove.'

'What time did you and Mrs Redfern leave?'

'She said she'd wait for me in the hall at half past ten. I was afraid I was going to be late, but it was all right. I was about three minutes early.'

'And what did you do at Gull Cove?' asked Poirot.

'Oh, I oiled myself and lay in the sun, and Mrs Redfern did some drawing. Then I swam and Christine went back to the hotel to get ready for tennis.'

'Do you remember what time that was?' Weston asked.

'When Mrs Redfern went back to the hotel? Quarter to twelve.'

'Are you sure of that time – quarter to twelve?'

'Oh yes. I looked at my watch.'

'The watch you are wearing now? Do you mind if I see?'

He compared her watch with his own and with the hotel clock on the wall.

'Quite correct!' he said, smiling. 'So you had a swim? And you got back to the hotel – when?'

'At about one o'clock.' Her voice changed. 'And then I heard …'

'Did you – er – *like* Arlena?'

'Oh yes. Arlena was quite kind to me.'

'That's good,' said Weston. 'Sometimes a girl and her father are great friends and then she gets jealous of the new wife. You didn't feel like that?'

Linda stared at him, and said, 'Oh, no.'

'Sometimes there are arguments between husband and wife,' Weston continued, although he felt uncomfortable, 'that are difficult for a daughter too. Anything like that?'

'Oh, no,' said Linda. 'My father doesn't argue with people.'

'Now, Miss Linda,' said Weston, 'I want you to think very carefully. Have you any idea who killed Arlena? Do you know anything that could help us?'

Linda was silent and thoughtful for a minute. She said at last, 'No, I don't know who could possibly want to kill Arlena. Except Mrs Redfern. Her husband was in love with Arlena. But I don't think she really wanted to *kill* her. She probably just wanted her to be dead – and that isn't the same thing, is it?'

'No,' said Poirot gently, 'it is not at all the same.'

Linda nodded. 'Mrs Redfern could never kill somebody. She isn't *violent*.'

'I know what you mean, my child, and I agree with you,' said Poirot. 'She is not a very emotional person. She would not be …' He sat back with half closed eyes, and chose his words carefully, '… shaken by a storm of feeling – seeing a face she hated – a hated white neck – wanting to press her hands into it …'

Linda moved back from the table. 'Can I go now? Is that all?' she said, and her voice was shaking.

'Yes, yes, that's all. Thank you, Miss Linda,' said Weston. He got up to open the door for her and then came back to the table and lit a cigarette.

'Well,' he said, 'our job is not a nice one. I felt bad, asking that child about her father and his wife, but, we had to do it. Murder is murder. You said too much, I thought, Poirot, when you talked about hands and necks – not quite the sort of ideas to give to a child!'

'So,' said Poirot thoughtfully, 'you thought I put ideas into her head?'

'Well, you did, didn't you?' Poirot shook his head, but Weston continued. 'We got very little useful information from her, except an almost complete **alibi** for the Redfern woman. Goodbye to the jealous wife idea.'

'There are better reasons to leave Mrs Redfern out of it,' said Poirot. 'She isn't

---

alibi /ˈælɪbaɪ/ (n) information that proves that a person was not responsible for a crime because he or she was in another place at that time

strong enough in body or in mind to strangle anyone. And she is able to love and to be loyal, but she does not feel strong emotion.'

'Well,' said Weston, 'I suppose we'd better see the Redferns next.'

◆

Patrick Redfern was calm again now, but he looked pale and tired.

'How long had you known Mrs Marshall?'

'Three months.'

'Mr Marshall has told us that you met her at a party,' said Weston. 'Is that right?'

'Yes, that's how it happened.'

'Mr Marshall seemed to think that you didn't know each other well before you met again here. Is that true, Mr Redfern?'

'Well …' Patrick Redfern paused. 'Not exactly. Actually, I saw her quite often.'

'And Mr Marshall didn't know?'

Redfern's face went slightly red. 'I don't know whether he knew or not.'

'And did your wife also not know, Mr Redfern?' asked Poirot quietly.

'I believe I told my wife that I had met the famous Arlena Stuart.'

'Did you and Mrs Marshall arrange to meet down here?'

'Well,' said Redfern, after a silence, 'I suppose everyone knows that I was crazy about the woman – in love. She wanted me to come down here. I – I did anything she wanted. She had that effect on people.'

'You paint a very clear picture of her,' said Poirot. 'She was the famous *Circe**.'

'She certainly turned men into pigs!' Redfern agreed. 'I'm being honest with you, gentlemen. I'm not trying to hide anything. Why would I do that? I was in love with her. I don't know whether she cared for me. She pretended to, but I think she lost interest in men when she'd got them.'

Poirot sat forwards. 'And how do you feel now?'

Patrick Redfern looked straight into Poirot's eyes, 'I want to know this – how much does the public have to know? It's going to be quite bad for my wife. Oh, I know,' he continued quickly. 'You think I haven't thought much about her until now? Perhaps that's true. But I truly care for my wife – very deeply. The other thing was madness. But Christine is different. She's *real*. I've always known she was the person who really mattered. Please believe that.'

'But I do believe it. Yes, yes, I do,' Hercule Poirot said.

'If there's no connection between your relationship with Mrs Marshall and the murder,' said Weston, 'then nobody needs to know about it. But you must realise it could be very important. It could show us a motive for the crime. Mr Marshall, perhaps, *didn't* know about it. Imagine if he suddenly found out?'

---

* *Circe*: a magical character in old Greek stories, who had the power to turn men into pigs

'Oh, God!' said Redfern. 'Do you mean he found out and – and killed her?'

'Hadn't you thought of that?' asked the chief constable.

'No.' Redfern shook his head. 'It's strange. I never thought of it. Marshall's such a quiet man. I – oh, it doesn't seem likely.'

'What was Mrs Marshall's attitude to her husband?' asked Weston, 'Was she worried that he would find out? Or didn't she care?'

'She was a bit nervous,' said Redfern slowly. 'She didn't want him to know.'

'Did she seem afraid of him?'

'Afraid? No, I wouldn't say that.'

'Excuse me, Mr Redfern,' said Poirot, 'Did you ever think about divorce?'

'Oh no, never. There was Christine, you see. And Arlena, I'm sure, was satisfied with her marriage to Marshall. He's quite an important man ...' He smiled suddenly. 'And quite rich. She never thought of me as a possible *husband*. I knew that all the time, but it didn't change my feelings for her.'

'Did you have an appointment with Mrs Marshall this morning?'

'Not a special appointment, no. We usually met every morning on the beach.'

'Were you surprised when Mrs Marshall wasn't there this morning?'

'Yes, I was. Very surprised. I couldn't understand it at all.'

'What did you think?'

'Well, I didn't know what to think. All the time I thought she would come.'

'If she had another appointment, have you any idea who it was with?'

Patrick Redfern just stared and shook his head.

'When you had a *rendezvous** with Mrs Marshall,' Poirot asked, 'where did you meet?'

'Sometimes I used to meet her in the afternoon at Gull Cove. There's no sun there in the afternoon so there aren't usually many people there.'

'Never at the other cove? Pixy Cove?'

'No. We never tried to meet in the morning. People would notice. In the afternoon people go and sleep or just lie around and nobody knows where anyone else is. After dinner we used to go for a walk together.'

'Ah, yes!' said Poirot quietly, and Patrick Redfern looked at him, surprised.

'Then you cannot tell us why Mrs Marshall went to Pixy Cove this morning?'

Redfern shook his head and said, 'I have no idea!'

'Now, Mr Redfern, think very carefully. You knew Mrs Marshall in London. You must know some of her London friends. Do you know anyone who could be her enemy? Someone, for example, who was her lover before you?'

'Honestly,' said Patrick Redfern, 'I can't think of anyone.'

'Well,' said Weston, 'we are left with two people here with a motive. Her husband and your wife.'

'My wife? Christine? Do you mean that *Christine* was part of this? You're mad – completely mad – Christine? It's *impossible*. It's funny.'

'Jealousy is a very powerful motive, Mr Redfern,' said Weston. 'Jealous women can lose control of themselves completely.'

'Not Christine,' said Redfern. 'She was unhappy – but she isn't violent.' Hercule Poirot nodded thoughtfully. 'And another thing,' Redfern continued confidently. 'I doubt if Christine could strangle a cat – or climb down the ladder to the beach – she can't do that kind of thing.'

'Well,' said Weston, 'I suppose it doesn't seem very likely. But motive's the first thing we have to look for. Motive and opportunity.'

◆

When Redfern left the room, the chief constable said with a smile, 'I didn't think I needed to tell the man that his wife has an alibi.'

'His arguments were as good as an alibi,' said Poirot.

'Yes. She didn't do it. It's impossible, as you said. And it seems that Marshall didn't.'

'Excuse me, sir,' said Colgate, 'but I've been thinking about *his* alibi. It's possible that he'd thought about all this, and had prepared those letters *earlier*.'

'That's a good idea,' said Weston, 'We must find out …'

* *rendezvous*: French for *meeting*

He stopped talking as Christine Redfern entered the room. She was, as always, calm. She looked pretty in a pale way. But, thought Hercule Poirot, her face was not silly or weak. It was brave and sensible.

'Sit down, Mrs Redfern,' Weston said. 'We have to ask everybody to tell us what they did this morning. Just for our records.'

'Oh yes,' said Christine Redfern, 'I understand. Where shall I begin?'

'As early as possible,' said Poirot. 'What did you do when you got up?'

'On my way down to breakfast I went into Linda's room and arranged to go to Gull Cove this morning. We agreed to meet in the sitting-room at half past ten.'

'You did not swim before breakfast, Madame?'

'No, I rarely do.' She smiled. 'I like the sea warm.'

'But your husband swims then?'

'Oh yes. Nearly always.'

'And Mrs Marshall?'

Christine's voice changed. It became cold. 'Oh, no. Mrs Marshall never appeared before the middle of the morning.'

'Excuse me, Madame, I interrupted you. You were saying that you went to Linda Marshall's room. What time was that?'

'Hmm – half past eight – no, a little later.'

'And was Miss Marshall up then?'

'Oh yes, she'd been out. She said she'd been for a swim.' Christine sounded a little embarrassed. 'I went down to breakfast, and then I went upstairs, collected my drawing things and we left.'

'You and Miss Linda Marshall? What time was that?'

'It was half past ten. We went to Gull Cove. I drew and Linda lay in the sun.'

'What time did you leave the cove?'

'Quarter to twelve. I was playing tennis at twelve and I had to change my clothes. Linda stayed there and went swimming.'

'Did you have your watch with you?'

'No, actually I didn't. I asked Linda the time.'

'Were you sitting far from the sea?'

'Well, we were under the cliff – so I could be out of the sun and Linda in it.'

'Did Linda Marshall actually enter the sea before you left the beach?'

'Let me think,' said Christine thoughtfully. 'She ran down the beach – yes, I heard the sound of her in the waves as I was on the path.'

'Are you sure, Madame, that she really entered the sea?'

'Oh yes.' Christine Redfern and Weston both stared at Poirot. 'Then I went back to the hotel, changed my clothes and went to the tennis courts. We played two games. We were going in when we heard about Mrs Marshall.'

'And what did you think?' asked Poirot, sitting forwards.

'It was – a horrible thing,' said Christine Redfern slowly.

'Yes, but what did it mean to *you* – personally? You are an intelligent woman, Madame. I am sure you had formed an opinion of Mrs Marshall?'

'I was not, perhaps, surprised. Shocked, yes. But she was the kind of woman …'

'… who might be murdered … Yes, Madame, that is the truest and most important thing that has been said today. What did you really think of her?'

'Well, what shall I say?' Her pale face was suddenly red. 'She had no value at all. She did nothing useful. She had no mind – no brains. She only thought about men and clothes and being admired. She was attractive to men, of course. I wasn't surprised by the way she died. She was the sort of woman who experiences the worst things – **blackmail**, jealousy, violence.'

She stopped, and Weston suddenly realised what she had said.

'Why, when you were speaking about Arlena, did you use the word *blackmail*?'

blackmail /ˈblækmeɪl/ (n/v) the crime of making someone do something so their secrets are not told

41

4.1 Were you right?

Look back at your answers to Activity 3.4. Then put in order these people's activities on the morning of the murder, according to their own statements.

a Kenneth Marshall

.... typed letters

.... found his wife's room empty

.... had breakfast

......*1*....... talked to Arlena

.... played tennis

.... swam

b Christine Redfern

.... went to Gull Cove

.... played tennis

.... visited Linda's room

.... had breakfast

4.2 What more did you learn?

At one point, Chief Constable Weston believes that two people have a motive.

1 Complete his notes.

time of murder?

earliest ....

latest ....

method?

strangled, probably

by someone with

....

Kenneth Marshall

motives: ....

.... and ....

....

alibi: ....

....

....

Christine Redfern

motive: ....

....

alibi: ....

....

....

2 Discuss whether there is any other important information about these people that should be added to the notes.

4.3 **Language in use**

Read the sentences in the box. Then complete the sentences below, using past simple and past perfect verb forms.

> '**Had** she **met** any of the guests in this hotel before you **came** here?'
>
> 'I **went** to my room, but the girl **hadn't finished** cleaning it.'

1 A lot of people ......*Knew*...... Arlena because she ......*had been*...... an actress. (know, be)

2 .... Arlena before they .... at the same hotel? (Patrick/meet, stay)

3 Rosamund .... Kenneth because they . ... together. (recognise, grow up)

4 Linda's mother .... before Kenneth .... Arlena. (die, marry)

5 Kenneth .... his letters, so they .... still in his pocket. (not post, be)

6 Where .... before she .... breakfast? (Linda/be, have)

4.4 **What happens next?**

Guess who is speaking. Write the correct letters.

| A | B | C | D | E |

Mrs Gardner   Mr Gardner   Poirot   Major Barry   Stephen Lane

1 .... 'Yes, dear.'

2 .... 'Since I arrived, I have felt evil around us.'

3 .... 'I've travelled around and learnt a lot about human nature.'

4 .... 'So I was right. But the other thing – is that possible?'

5 .... 'Nothing is needed except strength – and the heart of a killer!'

6 .... 'We had no idea what was happening on that lonely beach.'

CHAPTER 7

Blackmail

'I've always said that there was something evil about that woman. And you see, I've been proved right.'

'I heard something.' Christine's face was pink. 'I didn't mean to. Three nights ago, we were playing cards. My husband and I, Monsieur Poirot and Miss Darnley. I went outside for some fresh air and I heard Arlena's voice. She said, "I can't get any more money now. My husband will suspect something." And then a man said, "You have to pay." Arlena said, "You evil blackmailer!" He said, "Evil or not, you'll pay." Then Arlena rushed past, looking very upset.'

'And the man?' said Weston. 'Do you know who he was?'

'He kept his voice low. It could be anyone.'

◆

'Now we're making progress!' said Colgate, when the door had closed behind Christine Redfern. 'Somebody in this hotel was blackmailing the lady.'

'But it is not the evil blackmailer who lies dead,' said Poirot quietly. 'It is the person he was blackmailing.'

'Yes, that's a bit of a problem, but it's a reason for Mrs Marshall's strange behaviour this morning. She had a meeting with the blackmailer. And they chose the perfect place.'

'Yes,' said Poirot. 'It is empty, and from the land you can only get down there by a ladder. In addition, you cannot see most of the beach because the cliff hangs over it. And there is a cave there. Someone could hide and wait.'

'We'd better look inside it,' said Colgate. 'We might find something.'

'Yes,' Weston agreed. 'We've got the answer to part one of the mystery: *Why did Mrs Marshall go to Pixy Cove?* But we want the other half too: *Who did she go there to meet?* I suppose it was someone staying at the hotel. None of the other men seems to be a possible lover – but a blackmailer, perhaps. We have Gardener, Barry, Blatt and Lane.'

'The American was on the beach all morning. That's right, isn't it, Poirot?'

'He was only absent for a short time when he fetched some wool for his wife.'

'Major Barry went out at ten,' said Colgate. 'He returned at one thirty. Reverend Lane had breakfast at eight. He said he was going for a walk. Mr Blatt went sailing at nine thirty. Neither of them is back yet.'

'Sailing, eh?' said Weston thoughtfully.

'It might fit rather well,' said Colgate.

'We'll talk to Major Barry later,' said Weston. 'Who else is there? Rosamund Darnley. And Miss Brewster, who found the body with Redfern. What's she like?'

'She's a sensible woman,' said Colgate. 'I don't think she'll have anything more to tell us, but we have to make sure. Then there are the Americans.'

'Let's talk to them all soon,' said Weston. 'We might learn something – about the blackmail, at least.'

◆

Mr and Mrs Gardener came into the room together.

'I hope you'll understand,' said Mrs Gardener immediately. 'This has been a very bad shock to me, and Mr Gardener is always very careful of my health …'

'Mrs Gardener feels things very deeply,' said Mr Gardener.

'… and he said to me, "I'm coming with you." Of course, we greatly admire the British police. Once I lost some jewellery and the young man was lovely, and …'

Weston spoke quickly. 'Were you both on the beach all morning?'

'Certainly we were,' said Mrs Gardener. 'It was a lovely peaceful morning. We had no idea what was happening round the corner on that lonely beach.'

'Did you see Mrs Marshall today?'

'We did not. I said to Odell, "Where is Mrs Marshall this morning?" And first her husband was looking for her and then that good-looking young man, Mr Redfern. He was on the beach looking angry. I said to myself, "Why, when he has that nice pretty little wife, must he run after that awful woman?" That's what I thought she was. I always thought that, didn't I, Odell?'

'Yes, dear.'

'I can't imagine why that nice Mr Marshall married such a woman, and when he has that nice young daughter. A more sensible choice would be Miss Darnley. She's a lovely woman and a very special one. You can see that she has brains. She could plan and do anything she liked. I admire her. And I said that she was clearly in love with Mr Marshall, didn't I, Odell?'

'Yes, dear.'

'It seems they knew each other as children, and now it might be all right, with that woman out of the way. I've always said that there was something evil about that woman. And you see, I've been proved right.'

Hercule Poirot's lips smiled slightly and his eyes met Mr Gardener's.

'Have either of you noticed anything that might help us?' said Weston.

'Well, no, I don't think so.' Mr Gardener spoke slowly. 'Mrs Marshall was with young Redfern most of the time – but everybody can tell you that.'

'What about her husband? Did he mind, do you think?'

'Mr Marshall is a quiet, shy man,' said Mr Gardener carefully.

'Yes,' said Mrs Gardener, 'He is so British!'

◆

Major Barry was trying to look upset but he also seemed to be enjoying himself.

'I'm glad to help you in any way I can,' he said. 'Of course I don't know anything about it, but I've travelled around and learnt a lot about human nature. This reminds me of a man called Robinson. A quiet man. He attacked his wife one evening – held her by the throat – because she'd been with another man. He nearly killed her! It surprised us all.'

'Do you think this is like the death of Mrs Marshall?' asked Hercule Poirot.

'Well, I mean – strangled. A man suddenly goes mad with anger!'

'Do you think Mr Marshall felt like that?' said Poirot.

'Oh, I never said that.' Major Barry's face went even redder. 'Marshall's a very nice man. I wouldn't say anything bad about him.'

'*Pardon**, but you *were* talking about the behaviour of a husband.'

'Well, I imagine she'd had a lot of admirers. Husbands are stupid. They see a man likes their wife, but they don't see that *she* likes *him*. It reminds me ...'

'Yes, yes, Major Barry,' said Weston. 'We just have to discover the facts. Have you seen or noticed anything that might help us?'

'No, I haven't, not really. I saw her and young Redfern one afternoon on Gull Cove.' He laughed. 'But you don't want that kind of evidence. Ha ha!'

'You didn't see Mrs Marshall this morning?'

'I didn't see anybody this morning. I went to St Loo. That's typical of my luck. Nothing happens for months – then, when it does, you miss it!'

* *pardon*: French for *sorry*

46

'Did you say you went to St Loo?'

'Yes, I wanted to make some phone calls. There's no telephone here and the post office on the mainland isn't very private. I wanted to phone a friend about a horse race – put some money on a horse. I couldn't get through to him, unfortunately.'

'Where did you telephone from?'

'The post office in St Loo. Then on the way back I got lost – these stupid little country roads. I wasted an hour, at least. I only got back half an hour ago.'

'Did you speak to anyone or meet anyone in St Loo?' Weston asked.

'Do you want an alibi?' laughed Major Barry. 'I saw about fifty thousand people in St Loo – but that doesn't mean they'll remember me. The newspapers will call this The Lonely Beach Murder. That reminds me …'

Inspector Colgate stopped the story and showed the major out of the room.

'It's difficult to check anything in St Loo. It's the holiday season.'

'Yes,' replied Weston. 'We can't take him off the list, but I don't seriously think it was him. Check what time he took the car out, and the petrol. It's possible that he parked somewhere lonely, walked back here and went to the cove. But I don't think so – too dangerous. He could be seen.'

'There are quite a lot of tour buses here today,' said Colgate, 'It's a fine day. They usually start arriving at about half past eleven. Low tide was at about one o'clock. People were probably all over the beach and all round the island.'

'Yes,' said Weston. 'He'd have to come up from the mainland past the hotel.'

'Not right past it. He could take the path that goes over the top of the island. But perhaps he went round to the cove by boat.'

'That's much more likely. He could have a boat ready, leave the car, row to Pixy Cove, murder Arlena, row back, pick up the car and then say he'd been to St Loo and got lost. It would be hard to prove that story was wrong. I'll let you check, Colgate. You know what to do. We'd better see Miss Brewster now.'

After Emily Brewster had repeated her story, Weston said, 'And you know nothing else that could help us?'

'I'm afraid not,' said Emily Brewster. 'It's a horrible business, but I expect you'll solve it. It oughtn't to be too difficult.'

'What do you mean, Miss Brewster?'

'I just mean, with a woman like that it ought to be easy enough. You can't get away from *facts*. She was bad. Just look at her unpleasant past.'

'You did not like her?' asked Hercule Poirot gently.

'No – I know too much about her. My cousin married one of the Erskine family. That woman made old Sir Robert leave most of his money to her.'

'And the family – er – were upset?'

'Of course. Her relationship with him was embarrassing, and then he left her fifty thousand pounds. It shows what kind of woman she was. I know about someone else, too – a young man who was completely crazy about her. He did something illegal and nearly went to prison, just to get some money to spend on her. That woman had a bad effect on everyone she met. She was ruining young Redfern. No, I'm afraid I'm not sorry about her death – although of course strangling is rather unpleasant.'

'And do you think the murderer was someone from her past?'

'Yes, I do.'

'Someone who came from the mainland, and wasn't seen?'

'Why would anyone see him? We were all on the beach. The Marshall child and Christine were at Gull Cove, and Mr Marshall was in his room. Who could see him, except possibly Miss Darnley? She was at Sunny Ledge. Mr Redfern and I saw her there, when we were rowing round the island.'

◆

'She really disliked the dead lady, didn't she?' said Colgate, thoughtfully, when Miss Brewster had left. 'It's a pity she has a perfect alibi for the whole morning. Did you notice her hands? As big as a man's. She's a big woman – stronger than many men. You say she never left the beach this morning, Monsieur Poirot?'

'My dear man, she came down to the beach before Mrs Marshall reached Pixy Cove, and I could see her until she left with Mr Redfern in the boat.'

'Then she's off the list too,' said Colgate sadly. He seemed upset about it.

♦

As usual, Hercule Poirot was very pleased to see Rosamund Darnley.

'Now, Miss Darnley, what did you do this morning?' Weston asked.

'I had breakfast at about nine thirty. Then I went upstairs to collect some books and my sun umbrella, and went out to Sunny Ledge. That was at about twenty-five past ten. I came back at about twenty to twelve, got my tennis things and went out to the courts, where I played tennis until lunch time.'

'Did you see Mrs Marshall this morning?'

'No.'

'Did you see her from the cove as she went past in her boat?'

'No, she had probably gone past before I got there.'

'Did you notice *anyone* in a boat this morning?'

'No, I don't think so. I was reading.'

'You and Mr Marshall knew each other before, I think?'

'Mr Marshall is an old family friend. I hadn't seen him for many years.'

'And Mrs Marshall?'

'I hadn't really spoken to her before I came here.'

'Did Mr Marshall love his wife, do you think?'

'Perhaps. I can't really tell you anything about that.'

'Did you like Mrs Marshall, Miss Darnley?'

'Arlena Marshall was not popular with other women, but she dressed well and she always looked good.'

'Did she spend a lot on clothes?'

'I think so. She had her own money, and of course Mr Marshall is quite rich.'

'Did you ever think that she was being blackmailed, Miss Darnley?'

'Blackmailed? Why would anyone blackmail Arlena?'

'There are some things that she might not want her husband to know?'

'Well, yes …' She half smiled. 'I sound doubtful, but, you see, everyone knew about Arlena's behaviour. She never pretended to be different.'

'Do you think her husband knew about her – friendships with other people?'

'I don't really know what to think. I've always thought that Kenneth Marshall accepted his wife as she was. But that may not be true.'

'And you know of no one who was likely to be her enemy?'

'Only jealous wives – but I suppose, because she was strangled, a man killed her. No, I can't think of anyone. But you'll have to ask her friends.' She smiled at Poirot. 'Hasn't Monsieur Poirot any questions to ask?'

Poirot shook his head and smiled. 'I can think of nothing,' he said.

Rosamund Darnley stood up and went out.

CHAPTER 8

'That's Strange!'

'So I was right. But the other thing – is that possible too?
No, it is not, unless ... unless ...'

The three men were standing in Arlena Marshall's bedroom. The sun shone onto the bottles and jars on the table. Inspector Colgate found a packet of letters, and he and Weston looked through them together. Hercule Poirot had moved to the cupboard. He looked at the many dresses and suits.

'*Les femmes!*' he said with a faint smile.

'Three letters from young Redfern,' said Weston. 'He'll learn he shouldn't write letters to women. They always keep them. There's one other letter here.' He held it out to Poirot.

Dearest Arlena, I feel so sad. I am going to China and I won't see you for years. I am so crazy about you! Thanks for the money. I won't go to prison now. Can you forgive me? I wanted to give you jewellery. Yes, jewels for your beautiful ears, your lovely throat. Don't forget me – but I know you won't. You're mine – always.

Goodbye – goodbye – goodbye.

JN

'We'd better check if JN really went to China,' said Colgate, 'He might be the person we're looking for. Crazy about her, finds out she's made a fool of him. I think he might be the boy Miss Brewster was talking about.'

Poirot nodded. 'Yes,' he said. 'That letter is very important.'

He turned and stared at the room. Then they went into Kenneth Marshall's room. On the wall between the two windows was a mirror. In one corner was a little table, with a hair brush, a clothes brush and a bottle of hair cream. In another corner was a desk. On it was a typewriter and a pile of papers. Colgate looked through them quickly.

'It all seems fine,' he said. 'Here's the letter he was replying to. The date is 24th – that's yesterday. And here's the envelope, with its postmark. Now we'll be able to check the story he told us.'

They went into Linda's room. 'I don't suppose there's anything to see here,' said Weston. 'Perhaps Marshall hid something here. But it isn't likely.'

Weston went out again, but Hercule Poirot stayed behind. He found something that interested him in the fireplace. Something had been burnt there recently. He bent down and worked patiently. He found a piece of candle, some small pieces of green paper or cardboard (possibly from a notebook), and some printed words ... *not dream them* ... There was also an ordinary pin and something that was possibly burnt hair. Poirot stared at them.

'"Do great things, not dream them all day long". *C'est possible.**'
Then he picked up the pin and his eyes grew brighter.
'*Pour l'amour de Dieu†! Is it possible?'
He looked slowly round the room. Near the fireplace were some shelves with
a row of books. Poirot noticed a book behind the others – a small brown leather
book. He took it and opened it. Very slowly, he nodded his head.

'So I was right. But the other thing – is that possible too? No, it is not, unless
… unless …'

The room next to Linda's was the Redferns'. Poirot looked into it, and
noticed the signs of two different kinds of people – Christine, who was very tidy,
and Patrick, who was not. Nothing else interested him in the room.

The next room was Rosamund Darnley's, and he stayed here for a moment
just to enjoy the pleasure of the owner's personality. He noticed the books
and the expensive creams and make-up. He could sense the faint, expensive
perfume that Rosamund Darnley used. Her room was the last one. Next to it
was a balcony, with steps down to the rocks. Hercule Poirot stepped outside and
looked down. Below, there was a path down to the rocks and the sea. There was
also a path round the hotel to the left.

* *c'est possible*: French for *it's possible*
† *pour l'amour de Dieu*: French for *for the love of God*, showing the speaker's surprise

perfume /ˈpɜːfjuːm/ (n/v) a liquid with a pleasant smell that you put on your skin

'One could go down these stairs, round the hotel and then join the main path to the mainland,' he said.

Weston nodded, and added, 'You could go right across the island without going through the hotel. But someone might see you, through a window. Some of the public bathrooms look out that way – north. Also the games room.'

'You can't see through the bathroom windows,' said Poirot, 'and one does not play indoor games on a fine morning.'

'Exactly,' said Weston. 'If Mr Marshall did it, that's the way he went. Blackmail or no blackmail, I still think it was him. His behaviour is odd.'

'Perhaps,' said Hercule Poirot, 'but that does not make him a murderer.'

'So you're sure it's not him?'

'No.' Poirot shook his head. 'I would not say that.'

'We'll see what Colgate decides about the typing alibi. Let's talk to the servant who cleans this floor. Her evidence may be important.'

The servant was confident and intelligent. Mr Marshall had come up to his room not long after ten thirty and he had asked her to be as quick as possible. She had not seen him come back but she had heard the typewriter a little later – at about five to eleven, when she was in Mr and Mrs Redfern's room. Then she had moved to Miss Darnley's room – at just after eleven. She remembered hearing the church clock. At quarter past eleven she had gone downstairs for a rest. Then she had cleaned the other rooms in this order:

Linda Marshall's, the two public bathrooms, Mrs Marshall's bedroom and bathroom, Mr Marshall's room, Miss Darnley's bedroom and bathroom.

During the time she had been in Miss Darnley's rooms, she had not heard anyone pass the door or go out by the stairs to the rocks, although it was possible that someone had passed her very quietly.

No, Mrs Marshall hadn't usually got up early. She, Gladys Narracott, had been surprised to find the door open and Mrs Marshall gone at just after ten.

No, she hadn't noticed anything unusual about Mrs Marshall that morning.

'What did you think of Mrs Marshall, Mademoiselle?' asked Poirot quietly. Gladys Narracott stared at him. 'We would be interested – very interested – in your opinion.'

Gladys looked anxiously at the chief constable, who smiled and nodded, although he felt slightly embarrassed by the foreign detective's methods.

'Well, she wasn't exactly a lady. I mean, she was more like an actress.'

'She *was* an actress,' said Weston.

'Yes, that's what I mean. She did exactly what she felt like doing. She didn't worry about being polite. She used to be friendly sometimes and then rude and nasty at other times. None of us *liked* her. But her clothes were beautiful. And of course she was very good-looking, so she was admired.'

'I'm sorry to ask you this,' said Weston, 'but it is very important. Can you tell me about her relationship with her husband?'

'You don't – it wasn't – you don't think he did it?'

'Do you?' asked Poirot quickly.

'Oh! I wouldn't like to think so. He's such a nice gentleman, Mr Marshall. He couldn't do a thing like that – I'm sure he couldn't.'

'But you are *not* very sure – I can hear it in your voice.'

'You read things like this in the newspapers! When there's jealousy. And of course everyone's been talking about her and Mr Redfern. And Mrs Redfern is such a nice, quiet lady! It's a pity. And Mr Redfern's a nice, quiet gentleman too, but it seems that men can't control themselves with ladies like Mrs Marshall. If Mr Marshall found out about it …'

'Yes?' said Weston.

'I thought sometimes that Mrs Marshall was frightened of her husband. He's a very quiet gentleman but he isn't – he isn't *easy*.'

'But you don't know anything definite? Nothing they said to each other?' Gladys Narracott shook her head. 'What can you tell me about the letters that Mrs Marshall received this morning?'

'There were about six or seven, sir. I got them from the office as usual and took them up with her breakfast. They looked ordinary. Some were bills, I think – she threw them away. A policeman is looking through the rubbish now.'

'Well, I think that's all,' said Weston, but then Poirot spoke.

'When you cleaned *Linda* Marshall's room, did you clean the fireplace?'

'There wasn't anything to do. There hadn't been a fire.'

'What time did you clean her room?'

'At about quarter past nine, when she'd gone down to breakfast.'

'Did she come up to her room after breakfast? Do you know?'

'Yes, she came up at about quarter to ten. Then she hurried out again, rather quickly, just before half past ten.'

'You didn't go into her room again?'

'No, I'd finished with it.'

'There is another thing that I want to know,' said Poirot. 'Who went swimming before breakfast this morning?'

'Well, Mr Marshall and Mr Redfern were the only ones this morning, I think. Their wet swimsuits were hanging over the balcony as usual.'

'Miss Linda Marshall did not swim this morning?'

'No. All her swimsuits were dry.'

'Ah,' said Poirot. 'That is what I wanted to know. I wonder if you have noticed a bottle missing from any of the rooms? Would you notice?'

'I wouldn't from Mrs Marshall's room. She has so many. I'm not sure about Miss Darnley. She has quite a lot of creams and things. But from the other rooms, yes, I would. I mean, if I looked specially.'

'Perhaps you would go and look now.'

'Certainly,' said Gladys Narracott, and she left the room.

Weston looked at Poirot. 'What's this?' he asked.

'My tidy mind is worried by small things. Miss Brewster, this morning, was swimming off the rocks before breakfast. She said that a bottle was thrown from the rocks and nearly hit her. I want to know who threw that bottle, and why.'

'My dear man, it could be anyone.'

'Not at all. It was thrown from one of the rooms we have just examined. If you have an empty bottle, you do not go on to your balcony and throw it into the sea! You would only do that *if you did not want anyone to see that bottle.*'

Weston stared at him and said, 'Are you going to tell me now that Arlena Marshall wasn't strangled, but poisoned with a drug from a mysterious bottle?'

'No, no. I do not think there was poison in that bottle.'

'Then what was in it?'

'I do not know. That is why I am interested.'

Gladys Narracott came back. She was a little breathless. 'I'm sure that nothing has gone from Mr Marshall's room, or Miss Linda's room, or Mr and Mrs Redfern's room, and I'm almost sure there's nothing missing from Miss Darnley's either. But I'm sorry, I can't say about Mrs Marshall's.'

'It does not matter,' said Poirot. 'Are you sure there is nothing that you have forgotten to tell us? Perhaps something that made you think, "That's strange!"?'

'Well,' said Gladys doubtfully, 'not the sort of thing that you mean.'

'You do not know what I mean. Have you said to yourself or to a colleague today, "That is strange!"?'

'It was nothing really,' said Gladys. 'Just bath water running. I said to Elsie, downstairs, it was strange that somebody was having a bath at twelve o'clock.'

'Whose bath? *Who* was having a bath?'

'I don't know. We heard the water running from this part of the building.'

'You're sure it was a bath?'

'Oh, yes. You can't mistake the sound of bath water running away.'

Poirot showed no more desire to keep her, so Gladys was allowed to leave.

'You don't think the bath water is important, do you, Poirot?' asked Weston, 'I mean, there's no blood to wash off. That's the ...' He paused.

'That is the advantage of strangling!' Poirot said. 'No blood, no instrument, nothing to hide! Nothing is needed except strength – and the heart of a killer!'

His voice was so full of feeling that Weston stepped back a little.

Poirot smiled. 'It is probably not important. Perhaps Mrs Redfern had a bath before she played tennis, or Mr Marshall, or Miss Darnley.'

A policeman knocked on the door, and looked in.

'Miss Darnley would like to see you again. She forgot to tell you something.'

'We're coming down – now,' Weston said .

◆

Colgate was the first person they saw. He looked serious.

'I've been checking the typing story. There's no doubt – the typing couldn't be done in less than an hour. That seems to prove the alibi. And look at this letter: *My dear Marshall, sorry to worry you on your holiday but something unexpected has happened with the Burley and Tender business …* It's dated the 24th – that's yesterday. It was posted in London yesterday evening. The same typewriter was used for the envelope and the letter. The letter is quite complicated and it was impossible for Marshall to write his reply before he received it.'

'So Marshall seems to be innocent,' said Weston sadly. 'I must see Miss Darnley again. She's waiting now.'

'I'm really very sorry,' said Rosamund, 'but it probably isn't important. I told you that I spent the morning on Sunny Ledge. That isn't quite right. I forgot that once I went back to the hotel and out again.'

'What time was that, Miss Darnley?'

'About quarter past eleven, I think. I'd forgotten my sunglasses.'

'You went straight to your room and out again?'

'Yes. Well, actually, I just looked into Ken's – Mr Marshall's room. I heard his typewriter and I thought he was stupid to stay inside on such a lovely day.'

'And what did Mr Marshall say?'

'Well ...' Rosamund looked a little embarrassed. 'When I opened the door, he was working so hard that I just went away. I don't think he saw me.'

'And what time was that, Miss Darnley?'

'About twenty past eleven. I noticed the clock in the hall as I went out again.'

◆

'That proves it,' said Colgate. 'The servant heard him typing until five to eleven. Miss Darnley saw him at twenty past, and the woman was dead at quarter to twelve. He says he spent that hour typing in his room, and it seems to be true.' He paused. 'Monsieur Poirot looks very serious.'

'I was wondering why Miss Darnley suddenly offered this extra evidence.'

'Do you suspect she didn't just "forget"?' said Colgate slowly. 'Imagine that Miss Darnley wasn't on Sunny Ledge this morning, and somebody saw her somewhere else. She invents this story quickly, to explain her absence from Sunny Ledge. She was careful to say that Mr Marshall didn't see her.'

'Yes,' said Poirot quietly. 'I noticed that.'

'Do you remember what Mrs Gardener said?' Colgate said. 'She thought that Miss Darnley was rather fond of Mr Marshall. There'd be a motive there.'

'Arlena Marshall wasn't killed by a woman,' said Weston impatiently. 'We have to look for a man. We'd better see how long it takes to go from the hotel to the top of the ladder, running and walking. And up and down the ladder. And check the time it takes to go by boat from the beach to the cove.'

Inspector Colgate nodded. 'I'll do that now, sir,' he said confidently.

'I think I'll go to the cove,' said the chief constable. 'We ought to see if anyone was waiting in that Pixy Cave. I suppose the local people know about the place?'

'I don't think younger people do,' said Colgate. 'Since this has been a hotel, the coves have been private property. Nobody local goes there.'

'We could take Redfern with us,' said Weston. 'He told us about the cave. Are you coming, Monsieur Poirot?'

'I am like Miss Brewster and Mrs Redfern. I do not like going down ladders.'

'We can go there by boat.'

'My stomach – it is not happy on the sea.'

'Don't worry, it's a beautiful day. The sea is calm. You must come.'

Hercule Poirot looked doubtful, but at that moment Mrs Castle arrived.

'I hope I'm not interrupting,' she said, 'but Reverend Lane has just returned. And I don't know if it's important, but ...'

'Yes, yes?' said Weston impatiently.

'A lady and a gentleman were here at about one o'clock. They came from the mainland for lunch. They were informed that there'd been an accident and that lunch wasn't being served.'

'Any idea who they were?'

'None at all. They asked about the accident, but I couldn't tell them anything. They seemed to be summer visitors of the better class.'

'Well, thank you,' said Weston, 'Ask Reverend Lane to come in.'

◆

'I'm Chief Constable Weston,' Weston told Stephen Lane. 'I suppose you've been told what's happened?'

'Yes – oh, yes. Terrible … Terrible …' His thin body shook. He said in a low voice, 'Since I arrived, I have felt evil around us. We have stopped believing in evil, but it has never been more powerful than it is today!'

'That's *your* special subject. Mine is more ordinary – solving a murder.'

'Murder! An awful word,' said the reverend. 'One of man's earliest crimes against God, killing an innocent brother without pity …' He paused, his eyes half closed. Then, in a more normal voice he said, 'How can I help you?'

'First, can you tell us what you did today?'

'I walked to St Petrock-in-the-Combe, about ten kilometres from here. The church is very interesting.'

'Thank you, Reverend. Did you meet anyone on your walk?'

'Not to speak to. A couple of boys on bicycles and some cows. But I wrote my name in the visitors' book at the church.'

'Do you know anything that would help us in any way?'

'All I can tell you is this: I knew when I first saw her that there was evil around Arlena Marshall. She was evil! Now – she has been struck down!'

'Not struck down,' said Poirot. '*Strangled.* By a pair of *human* hands.'

'That's horrible – horrible. Must you say it like that?'

'It is simply what happened. Have you any idea whose hands they were?'

The other man shook his head.

'I know nothing – nothing …'

'Well,' said Weston, 'we must go to the cove.'

'Is that where – it happened? Can – can I come with you?'

'Certainly,' said Poirot. 'Come with me by boat. We start immediately.'

5.1 Were you right?

Look back at your answers to Activity 4.4. Then read this police report and circle five mistakes.

> ### Mr and Mrs Gardener
> They saw Arlena Marshall on the beach on the morning of the murder. Mrs Gardener didn't like Mrs Marshall. She thinks that Christine Redfern is in love with Kenneth Marshall.
>
> ### Major Barry
> He was not at the hotel this morning – he was shopping in St Loo. He thinks he is a good judge of character, and he believes that Arlena Marshall was killed by her husband.
>
> ### Reverend Lane
> He was out walking when the murder happened. He seems to think that Arlena Marshall was punished because she was 'evil'. He shows no interest in details of the murder.

5.2 What more did you learn?

Look at the pictures. Where are these found or noticed?

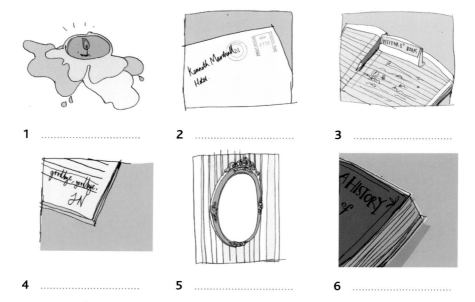

1 .... 2 .... 3 ....

4 .... 5 .... 6 ....

5.3 Language in use

Read the sentences in the box.
Then join the sentences below.
Use *who*, *which* or *that*, with or
without a comma.

'He could take **the path that** goes
over the top of the island.'

Gladys looked anxiously at **the chief
constable, who** smiled and nodded.

1 He's the man. He was at the hotel.

He's the man who/that was at the hotel.

2 This is the beach. I told you about it.

3 I saw the Marshalls. They were arguing.

4 Few visitors come to the island. It is often separated from the mainland.

5 We didn't talk to the other hotel employees. They weren't here at the time.

6 She has pale skin. It burns easily.

5.4 What happens next?

What do you think? Choose a, b or c.

1 At Pixy Cove, Poirot and the police find ...

   a someone hiding.   **b** some evidence.   **c** nothing useful.

2 Poirot finds out more about ...

   a the blackmailer.   **b** the bath.   **c** Marshall's alibi.

3 Linda Marshall is now ...

   a very sad.   **b** very frightened.   **c** much happier.

CHAPTER 9

A Trip to Pixy Cove

The police doctor came into the room. He looked excited.
'That's a nice little box of death you sent me.'

Patrick Redfern was rowing into Pixy Cove again. The other people in the boat were Poirot, very pale with a hand on his stomach, and Stephen Lane. Weston and two policemen were on the beach already. The three from the boat walked up to join them.

'Come and see what I've found on the beach,' said Constable Phillips.

Arranged on a rock were a pair of scissors, an empty cigarette packet, five bottle tops, some used matches, three pieces of string, one or two small pieces of newspaper, a piece of a broken pipe, four buttons, a chicken bone and an empty bottle of sun oil.

'Some of the things have been here for a long time,' said Weston. 'The scissors are new, though. *They* weren't out in yesterday's rain! Where were they?'

'Near the bottom of the ladder. Also this bit of pipe.'

'Mr Marshall told us he had lost his pipe,' said Poirot thoughtfully.

'Marshall's not our killer,' said Weston. 'And other people smoke a pipe.'

'You also smoke a pipe, don't you, Reverend Lane?' said Poirot.

'Oh, yes,' said the reverend. 'My pipe is an old friend.' He put his hand in his pocket again, took out his pipe, filled it with tobacco and lit it.

'I'm glad – they've taken *her* away ...' Redfern said in a low voice.

'Where was she found?' asked Stephen Lane.

'In the place where you're standing,' said Phillips cheerfully. Lane moved quickly away and stared down at it.

'The evidence shows that she arrived here at 10.45.' Weston turned to Redfern. 'Now, where's the entrance to this cave?'

Patrick Redfern was still staring at the place on the beach where Lane had been. Weston's words seemed to wake him. He led the way to a great pile of rocks. He went straight to two big rocks with a narrow space between them.

Weston squeezed through the space. Inside, there was more room. Poirot and Lane joined the chief constable. Colgate stayed outside. Daylight reached through the opening, but Weston had also brought a light with him.

'You'd never suspect it was here from outside,' said Weston. 'And the air is quite fresh – it doesn't smell of the sea.'

But to Poirot's nose, the air was more than fresh. It was perfumed. He knew two people who used that perfume ... He lifted his eyes to a small ledge.

'You are the tallest,' he said to Lane. 'Could you check that ledge?'

Lane stretched up his hands. 'There's a box here,' he said.

In a minute or two they were all out in the sunshine examining it. It was a dark green tin box with the word *Sandwiches* on it.

'I suppose it was left behind after a **picnic**,' said Phillips, and he opened it with his handkerchief. Inside were small containers marked *salt* and *pepper*, and two larger square tins for sandwiches. Phillips opened the salt container. It was completely full. 'There's salt in the pepper one too,' he said. Then he opened one of the bigger tins. That, too, contained the same white stuff. Very carefully, Phillips put a finger in and put it on his tongue. His face changed.

'This isn't *salt*. It has a bitter taste. It seems like some kind of *drug*.'

◆

'If drugs are part of this, there are several possibilities,' said Weston, back at the hotel. 'Do you think the dead woman was a gangster?'

'It is possible,' said Poirot carefully, 'but I doubt if she took drugs herself. She was very healthy. No, I don't think she took drugs.'

picnic /ˈpɪknɪk/ (n) an outdoor meal, especially in the country

'Perhaps she found out about this business by chance, and was silenced by these people. We'll know soon what exactly the stuff is. I've sent it for tests …'

Horace Blatt came quickly into the room. He was looking very hot.

'I've just heard the news! My name's Horace Blatt. Can I help you? I don't suppose so. I've been out in my boat since early this morning. Hello, Poirot. So you're working on this? I'll enjoy watching your detective work.'

Mr Blatt finally sat down, pulled out a cigarette case and offered it to Weston, who shook his head. 'I only smoke pipes.'

'Me too. I smoke cigarettes as well – but nothing's better than a pipe.'

'Then why not light your pipe?' asked Weston, but Blatt shook his head. 'I haven't got it at the moment,' he said. 'Tell me what's happening. I've only heard that Mrs Marshall was found murdered on one of the beaches here.'

'On Pixy Cove,' said Weston, watching him carefully.

'And was she strangled?' Mr Blatt asked excitedly.

'Yes, Mr Blatt.'

'Nasty – very nasty. Although I'm not surprised! Sexy woman – eh, Monsieur Poirot? Any idea who did it, or mustn't I ask?'

'You know, we are supposed to ask the questions,' said Weston with a faint smile. 'What time did you go sailing this morning, and was anyone with you?'

'I left here, alone, at quarter to ten. Went along the coast towards Plymouth.'

'Do you know anything about the Marshalls that might help?'

'I can only tell you that it wasn't me! The beautiful Arlena was nothing to me. She had her own admirer! And in my opinion Marshall knew about it. I saw him look angrily at young Redfern once or twice. Marshall seems like a quiet man but I've heard a few things about him. He was nearly sent to prison for attacking someone once – although it's true that the man had behaved quite badly. Marshall went crazy and half killed him.'

'So do you think it's possible that Marshall strangled his wife?' said Poirot.

'Not at all. I was just telling you that he could go crazy sometimes. This isn't a guess – it's certain … Redfern!'

'It was not Mr Redfern.'

Mr Blatt seemed surprised. He said slowly, 'Then I can't imagine … I'm sure it wasn't Mr Gardener – his wife controls him too much! That old fool Barry? Never! And it certainly wouldn't be the reverend. Although it's true, I have seen him watching her. A church man, but he likes the ladies!' Mr Blatt laughed, but stopped when he saw Weston's face. 'This will be in all the newspapers. The Jolly Roger won't be quite so high class in future.'

'You have not enjoyed your stay here?' asked Hercule Poirot.

'Well, no, I haven't. The sailing's all right and the views and the service and the food – but it isn't *friendly*. There's no *fun*.' He paused. His face was now very red. 'Don't listen to me. I get very upset.'

'And what do we think of Mr Blatt?' asked Hercule Poirot after he left.

Weston smiled. 'What do you think of him?'

'I think,' said Poirot, looking up at the ceiling, 'that he is – *nervous*.'

◆

'I've worked out those times,' said Colgate. 'From the hotel to the ladder, three minutes. That's walking until you're away from the hotel, and then running fast. Down the ladder to the beach, one and three-quarter minutes. Up the ladder, two minutes. Constable Flint is fit. If you walk and go down the ladder in the normal way, it would take about quarter of an hour.'

'There's another thing we must think about,' said Weston. 'The pipe.'

'Blatt smokes a pipe,' said Colgate. 'Marshall too, and the reverend. Redfern smokes cigarettes. Major Barry doesn't smoke at all. There's one pipe in Marshall's room, two in Blatt's, and one in Lane's. The servant says Marshall has two pipes. She doesn't know how many the others have.'

'Anything else?' asked Weston.

'Henry, in the bar, saw Marshall at ten to eleven, as Marshall said. William and George were outside. Neither was in a position to see someone coming across from the mainland.'

'Perhaps somebody came that way. But there's a new possibility, Colgate.'

Weston told him about the sandwich box in the cave.

'May I return these to you?' Colgate gave three letters to Marshall.

Kenneth Marshall smiled and said, 'Have the police been testing the speed of my typing? I hope you're satisfied.'

'Yes. Those letters take at least an hour to type. The servant heard you typing them until five to eleven, and you were seen by another witness at twenty past.'

'Really? That's good!'

'Yes, Miss Darnley came to your room at twenty past eleven. You were so busy typing that you didn't notice her.'

'Did she say that?' He paused. 'Actually, I *did* see her – in the mirror.'

'But you did not interrupt your writing?' Poirot asked.

'No. I wanted to finish it.'

As Kenneth Marshall went out, the police doctor came into the room. He looked excited.

'That's a nice little box of death you sent me. Diamorphine Hydrochloride*.'

'Ah!' said Inspector Colgate. 'Believe me, these drugs will give us the answer to the whole business.'

* Diamorphine Hydrochloride: a very dangerous and illegal drug

CHAPTER 10

Gabrielle Number 8

*'There are many colours and shapes, and every
strange little shape fits into its own place.'*

The little crowd of people came out of the courtroom.
Rosamund Darnley joined Kenneth Marshall. She said in a low voice,
'That wasn't so bad.' He did not answer at once. He knew that people were
staring at him. He had already met the reporters, and there had been cameras
everywhere.

'You must accept it, Ken. I know you like to stay unnoticed. But you are *the
husband of the murdered woman.*'

They walked away from the village. Eyes followed them but there was no one
very near. Rosamund Darnley's voice dropped as she repeated herself.

'It didn't really go so badly, did it?'

'I don't know. And I don't know what the police think.'

'That little man, Poirot – is he really interested in this?' said Rosamund
thoughtfully. 'He's quite old. He's probably lost his mind.'

They came to the coast on the mainland. Opposite them, calm in the
sunshine, lay the island. Rosamund spoke suddenly.

'Sometimes – things seem so unreal. I can't believe that it ever happened …'

'I think I know what you mean,' said Marshall slowly, 'Nature doesn't notice.
One insect fewer – that's all it is in nature!'

'Yes,' said Rosamund, 'and that's the right way to look at it, really.'

He looked at her and then he said in a low voice, 'Don't worry. *It's all right.*'

Linda came down to the shore to meet them. She seemed nervous and there were deep black shadows under her eyes. She spoke quickly.

'What happened, Father? What – what did they say?'

'Nothing. They'll meet again in two weeks. More evidence is needed.'

'But – but what do they think?'

'They aren't saying anything,' he said, and he started walking to the hotel.

Rosamund Darnley was following him when Linda called her name. She turned. The girl's unhappy face spoke to her. Rosamund took her arm and together they walked along the path to the end of the island.

'Try not to mind so much, Linda,' said Rosamund gently. 'I know it's terrible, and a shock. But you weren't *fond* of Arlena.'

Linda's body shook as she answered, 'No, I wasn't fond of her. But you don't understand. Christine doesn't understand either! Both of you have been nice to me, but you can't understand. If you knew what I know …'

Rosamund stopped suddenly. She stood for a minute or two, then took her arm from Linda's. 'What is it that you know, Linda?'

The girl stared at her. Then she shook her head. 'Nothing.'

Rosamund caught her arm. She held it tightly enough to hurt.

'Be careful, Linda. Be very careful.'

Linda's face had gone completely white. 'I am very careful – all the time.'

'Listen, *put the whole business out of your mind*. Never think about it. Forget … You can if you try! Arlena is dead. Nothing can bring her back to life. Forget everything and live in the future. And most importantly, *say nothing.*'

Linda moved back a little. She said, 'You … you seem to know all about it?'

'I don't know *anything*! In my opinion, a madman got onto the island and killed Arlena. That's the most likely solution. I'm almost sure the police will accept that. That's what probably happened. That's what *did* happen!'

'My mother was suspected of murder. Then my father married her. Perhaps he didn't think that murder was wrong.'

'Don't say things like that,' said Rosamund quickly, 'even to me! Your father has an alibi – an alibi that the police can't destroy. He's perfectly safe.'

'Did they think at first that my father …?' Linda whispered.

'I don't know what they thought! But they know now that he didn't do it. It's impossible. You can leave here soon. You'll forget everything!'

Linda spoke with sudden violence. *'I shall never forget.'*

◆

'There is something that I want to know, Madame.'

Christine Redfern looked up at Poirot. 'Yes?'

'It is something you said. You described how you went into Linda Marshall's room, found her absent, then how she returned. The chief constable asked you where she had been.'

'And I said she had been for a swim? Is that it?'

'But you did not say exactly that. Your words were, "She said she'd been for a swim." It is not the same! You answer shows what you were thinking. You were not sure that she *had* been for a swim. Why was that?'

'That's clever of you. It's true, I was a little surprised. I think it was the package in her hand. It was *candles* – they went all over the floor.'

'How did she behave – when the candles fell out of the package?'

'She was – upset,' said Christine slowly, 'and embarrassed.'

'Did you notice a notebook in her room? Possibly bright green?'

'A green notebook – rather a bright green. Yes, I have seen a notebook like that – but I can't remember where. Perhaps it was in Linda's room, but I can't be sure. What are you saying, Monsieur Poirot? What does all this mean?'

Poirot produced a small brown leather book. 'Have you seen this before?'

'I'm not sure – yes, Linda was looking at it in the village shop. But she put it back quickly when I came in. I wondered what it was.'

Silently Poirot showed the title: *A History of Magic and Poisons.*

'I don't understand,' said Christine. 'What does all this mean?'

'It may mean a lot,' said Poirot seriously. 'One more question, Madame. Did you have a bath that morning, before you went out to play tennis?'

'No. There was no time, and I didn't want a bath – not before tennis.'

Poirot nodded. 'It is not important,' he said.

◆

Hercule Poirot stood by the table where Mrs Gardener was trying to fit together the pieces of a **puzzle**. She looked up in surprise.

'Monsieur Poirot! Have you just come back from the court? The thought of it all makes me so nervous! I'm so upset. These puzzles make me calmer. Now, where *does* this white piece fit? I think it's part of the carpet, but …'

Gently, Poirot's hand took the piece from her.

'It fits, Madame, *here*. It is part of the cat.'

'No! That's impossible. It's a black cat.'

'A black cat, yes, but the end of the cat's tail is white.'

'Oh, yes! How clever of you! You know, I've been watching you. I wanted to watch a detective at work. That sounds rather heartless. Oh dear, every time I think of it I feel sick. I told Mr Gardener this morning that we must get away.

puzzle /ˈpʌzəl/ (n) a game that is difficult to do, especially one with pieces that fit together; a difficult problem

He thinks we can leave tomorrow. But I would really like to know your methods – could you *explain* them to me?'

'It is like your puzzle, Madame. One puts the pieces together. There are many colours and shapes, and every strange little shape fits into its own place.'

'That's so interesting! You explain it so beautifully!'

'One arranges the pieces very carefully and then a piece of one colour that should fit, for example, a carpet, fits instead a black cat's tail.'

'That is very interesting! And are there many pieces?'

'Yes, Madame. Almost everyone here in this hotel has given me a piece for my puzzle – including you. Something you said, Madame, was very helpful.'

'Well, that is so lovely! Can you tell me more, Monsieur Poirot?'

'Ah! Madame, I will explain at the end.'

◆

Poirot knocked gently on Mr Marshall's door. A short 'Come in!' came from the room and Poirot entered. Marshall's back was turned to him. He was typing at the table between the windows. His eyes met Poirot's in the mirror.

'A thousand apologies for interrupting. There is one little question. It is very simple. Only this. On the morning of your wife's death, did you have a bath after you finished typing and before you went out to play tennis?'

'A bath? No, of course I didn't! I'd had a swim only an hour earlier!'

'Thank you. That is all.' Poirot left the room, gently closing the door.

'The man's crazy!' said Kenneth Marshall to himself.

Just outside the bar, Poirot saw Mr Gardener. He was carrying two drinks. 'I shall be very glad to take my wife away,' said Mr Gardener in a low voice. 'This business is making her very nervous.'

'Will you allow me, Mr Gardener, to ask you one question? You are a man of the world. What, honestly, was your opinion of Mrs Marshall?'

Mr Gardener looked surprised. He looked carefully round and then said softly, 'Well, Monsieur Poirot, I've heard what people have been saying, especially the women, but I'll tell you my opinion – that woman was a fool!'

'Now that,' said Hercule Poirot, 'is very interesting.'

◆

Poirot sat down beside Rosamund Darnley on Sunny Ledge. Below them the sea was deep green and, further out, bright blue.

'Do you want to know what I think?' said Rosamund softly. 'I think you should look at the woman's past. Arlena was attractive to men. It's possible that she also got tired of them quickly. One of them was upset. He followed her here and killed her. He probably hid in the cave until he got his chance.'

'Would she go there to meet a man like that? No, she would not.'

'Perhaps he sent a message and used another person's name.'

'You forget one thing. It would be dangerous for a murderer to come across from the mainland and go past the hotel in daylight. Somebody might see him.'

'Perhaps they did. But I think it's quite possible that nobody noticed him.'

'It's *possible* – yes, I agree. But he could not be *sure* of it.'

'Aren't you forgetting something? The weather. The day of the murder was lovely, but the day before that there was rain and fog. That would hide someone's arrival on the island. Then he could spend the night in the cave.'

Rosamund's face went pink. 'That's my idea. Now tell me yours.'

'Ah, I am very simple. I usually believe that the most likely person is the criminal. From the beginning, one person seemed to be the most likely.'

'Yes?' said Rosamund coldly.

'But there is a problem. It seems that person *can't* be the murderer.' He heard her breathe out quickly. 'That is my problem. May I ask a question? When you came in to change for tennis that morning, did you have a bath?'

'A bath?' Rosamund stared at him. 'What do you mean?'

'That is what I mean. A bath. One gets in and gets out and then the water goes away!'

'Monsieur Poirot, are you completely mad? I *didn't* have a bath.'

'Ha!' said Poirot. 'So nobody had a bath. That is extremely interesting.'

'But why would anyone have a bath? You are being like Sherlock Holmes!'

'May I say, your perfume is lovely. Gabrielle Number 8, I think?'

'How clever you are. Yes, I always use it.'

'Mrs Marshall did too. It is fashionable, I suppose? And very expensive?'

Rosamund smiled, and Poirot said, 'You sat here, on the morning of the crime. You were seen here, or at least your sun umbrella was seen by Miss Brewster and Mr Redfern. During the morning, are you sure you did not go down to Pixy Cove and enter the cave there – the famous Pixy Cave?'

'Are you asking me if I killed Arlena Marshall?'

'No, I am asking you if you went into the Pixy Cave.'

'I don't even know where it is. Why would I go into it? For what reason?'

'On the day of the crime, Mademoiselle, somebody had been in that cave – somebody who used Gabrielle Number 8.'

'You've just said that Arlena Marshall used Gabrielle Number 8. She was on the beach there that day. I suppose she went into the cave. I've told you already that I never left this place the whole morning.'

'Except when you went to Mr Marshall's room,' Poirot reminded her.

'Yes, of course. I'd forgotten that.'

'You were wrong when you thought Mr Marshall hadn't seen you.'

'Kenneth saw me?' said Rosamund, surprised. 'Did he say that?'

'He saw you, Mademoiselle, in the mirror that hangs over the table.'

'Oh!' Poirot was looking at Rosamund Darnley's hands. They were well-shaped hands with very long fingers. She looked at him and said sharply, 'Why are you looking at my hands? Do you think … do you think …?'

'Do I think … what, Mademoiselle?'

'Nothing.'

◆

About an hour later, Poirot went to Gull Cove. There was someone sitting on the beach. He went down the path, walking carefully in his tight shiny shoes. Linda Marshall turned her head. He realised with pity how young she was.

'What is it? What do you want?'

'The other day you told us that you were fond of Arlena and that she was kind to you. That was not true, was it? I think you disliked her very much.'

'One can't say that when a person is dead. It wouldn't be very nice.'

'It is more important to discover the facts than to be very nice.'

'I want to forget it all. It's so horrible.'

'*But you can't forget, can you?* Will you let me help you, my child?'

Linda jumped up. 'I don't know what you are talking about.'

'I am talking about *candles* …'

He saw the frightened look in her eyes. She cried, 'I won't listen to you.'

She ran across the beach and up the path. Poirot shook his head sadly.

6.1 Were you right?

Look back at your answers to Activity 5.4. Then answer these questions.

1 What is being talked about?

a '*They* weren't out in yesterday's rain!' ....

b 'Mr Marshall told us he had lost *it*.' ....

c 'There's *something* up on this ledge.' ....

d '*This* isn't salt. *It* has a bitter taste.' ....

2 Answer the questions.

a Who heard Kenneth Marshall's typewriter? ....

b How long did his work probably take? ....

c Who else gives him his alibi? ....

3 Circle the sentence that is *not* true.

a Linda is worried about her father.

b She seems to have a terrible secret.

c She thinks that Rosamund is the murderer.

6.2 What more did you learn?

Who is speaking? Match the speech with the names. Then discuss with other students who or what each person is talking about.

1 'Don't say things like that, even to me!' ....

2 'That's impossible. It's a black cat.' ....

3 'Actually, I *did* see her – in the mirror.' ....

4 'that woman was a fool.' ....

5 'May I say, your perfume is lovely.' ....

6 'I won't listen to you.' ....

A **B**

Mrs Gardner   Kenneth Marshall

C **D**

Rosamund Darnley   Mr Gardner

E **F**

Linda   Poirot

6.3 Language in use

**Read the sentences in the box.
Then rewrite the sentences below,
using passive verb forms.**

'He **was** nearly **sent** to prison for attacking someone once.'

'More evidence **is needed**.'

1 They found Arlena's body at Pixy Cove.
Arlena's body was found at Pixy Cove.

2 They have just told her husband.
....

3 They are interviewing all the guests.
....

4 How did someone kill her?
....

5 People didn't like her.
....

6 They will report her death in all the newspapers.
....

7 They have found some letters.
....

8 They are examining the beach.
....

6.4 What happens next?

**Who might be the murderer, do you think? Discuss the possibilities with other
students and make notes on three characters below.**

Name	Motive(s)	Problems with alibi

CHAPTER 11

A Puzzle and a Picnic

His handsome face was changed – it was red and angry, the face
of a killer. He shouted, 'You horrible, stupid little man!'

Inspector Colgate was reporting to the chief constable. 'I've found out
something about Arlena's money, and it's a bit of a shock. You remember she
was left fifty thousand pounds by old Erskine? Well, there are only about fifteen
thousand left. She's been taking the money in cash. Blackmail.'

Weston nodded. 'And the blackmailer is here in the hotel. That means it's one
of those three men. Have you got any new information about any of them?'

'Major Barry used to be in the army, and he lives in a small flat – *but* he's
paid into the bank some very large sums of money this year. He says he's won it
at horse races. He certainly goes to the races. Next, Reverend Lane. He had to
give up his church about a year ago because of bad health – his mind, not his
body. He was in a special hospital. I think he was troubled by the idea of evil,
and especially evil in women. I think that Lane is at least a possibility. Perhaps
he felt it was his job to kill Mrs Marshall – that is, if he really *was* mad.'

'Nothing that fits with the blackmail idea?'

'No. He has money, but not very much, and no sudden increase recently.'

'What about his alibi?'

'Nobody remembers seeing him. In the book at the church, the name before
his was written three days earlier. It's possible he went there one or two days
before, and dated it the 25th.'

Weston nodded. 'And the third man?'

'Horace Blatt? There's definitely something odd there. He's been making
large sums of money for years – in ways that are not explained.'

'In fact, you think Mr Horace Blatt's profession is blackmailing?'

'Or drugs. I saw Chief Inspector Ridgeway, who's in charge of drug crime. It
seems that a lot of drugs have been coming into the country recently. He knows
who's selling them, but not how they get here.'

'If the Marshall woman's death is mixed up with drugs, we'd better let
Scotland Yard work on it. It seems the most likely possibility.'

'Yes, it does,' said Colgate unhappily, 'although I have some interesting
information. Marshall's business is in financial trouble. He thought that he'd get
fifty thousand pounds if his wife died. It seems a pity. He has two really good
motives for murder, but he can prove his innocence!'

'Don't worry, Colgate. We still have a chance to solve it. If a gangster killed
her, we've helped Scotland Yard to solve the drugs problem.'

An unwilling smile showed on Colgate's face. He said, 'Oh, I found out about the writer of the letter – the one signed JN. It doesn't help us. He's definitely in China – the same young man that Miss Brewster spoke of.'

'Right,' said Weston. 'Have you seen our Belgian colleague? Does he know everything you've told me?'

'He's a strange man, isn't he? Do you know what he asked me yesterday? He wanted details of any recent murders where people had been strangled.'

'Oh, did he? Now, I wonder … When did Reverend Stephen Lane go into that hospital? There was a murder – a young woman found somewhere near Bagshot. She was going to meet her husband and never arrived. And there was what the newspapers called the Lonely Wood Mystery. Both in Surrey.'

'Surrey? And his church was in Surrey. I wonder …'

◆

Hercule Poirot sat on the grass at the highest point of the island. On his left was the ladder down to Pixy Cove. There were several rocks where someone could hide. Not much of the beach could be seen because the cliff hung over it. He nodded. The pieces of the puzzle were fitting into position: a morning on the beach a few days before Arlena's death; five things that people had said that morning; the evening of the card game; the evening before the crime, his conversation with Christine and the scene on his way back to the hotel; Gabrielle Number 8; scissors; a broken pipe; a bottle; a green notebook; candles; a mirror and a typewriter; some purple wool; a watch; bathwater.

There was evil on the island. Evil … He looked down at the piece of paper in his hands. *Nellie Parsons, strangled in a lonely wood. No evidence ever discovered. Alice Corrigan.* He read, very carefully, the details of Alice Corrigan's death.

Inspector Colgate joined him. 'I've been interested in those other murders for years. Especially one.'

'Alice Corrigan?'

'Alice Corrigan. I've been talking to the Surrey police. She was found strangled less than fifteen kilometres from where Nellie Parsons was found. Both places are less than fifteen kilometres from Reverend Lane's home.'

'Tell me more about the death of Alice Corrigan,' said Poirot.

'The Surrey police decided at first that her husband was the guilty man. Not much was known about him. Her family hadn't wanted her to marry him, she'd had some money and she'd left it all to him – but then they checked his alibi. The body was discovered by a walker – a strong fit young woman and a very good witness. She was a sports teacher. She noted the time she'd found the body – four fifteen – and said she thought the woman had been dead for about ten minutes. That fitted with the doctor's opinion.

'From three o'clock to ten past four, Edward Corrigan was on a train from London. Four other people sat near him. Then he took the bus, with two other train passengers. He got off at the café where he'd arranged to meet his wife, at four twenty-five. He ordered tea and waited until five, but then he got worried. He thought perhaps she'd had an accident.

'It's thought that she was attacked by a stranger. The local police connected her death with Nellie Parsons. They decided the same man was responsible for both crimes, but they never caught him – in fact they found no evidence at all.'

He paused, and then said slowly, 'And now, here's a third woman strangled – and a rather odd man from Surrey.' He stopped and looked hopefully at Poirot, who seemed to be talking to himself.

'... which pieces are the carpet and which are the cat's tail?'

'*What* did you say?' the inspector asked.

'I apologise. I was thinking my own thoughts. Tell me, if you suspect that someone is telling lies but you can't prove it, what do you do?'

'I think if you tell enough lies you'll make a mistake in the end.'

'Yes, that is true. But one might perhaps make a little test – a test of one little lie. If one proved that was a lie, one would know that the others were lies too!'

'Your mind works in a strange way, doesn't it? But I expect it'll be all right in the end. May I ask, why did you ask about these other murders?'

'This crime seemed to be very well performed. I wondered if, perhaps, it was not a first try. I said to myself, let us examine past crimes that are similar.'

'You mean using the same method of killing?'

'No, I mean more than that. The death of Nellie Parsons tells me nothing. But the death of Alice Corrigan – do you not notice one thing that is very similar?'

'No, not really. Except that in each murder the husband has a perfect alibi.'
'Ah, so you *have* noticed that?'

◆

'Poirot – glad to see you. Come in. I think I've decided what to do,' said the chief constable, 'but I'd like your opinion. I've decided to ask Scotland Yard to join us. I think drug smuggling is at the heart of the whole business. And I'm almost sure who our drug smuggler is. Horace Blatt.' Poirot nodded. 'I can see that our minds have both worked the same way,' Weston continued. 'Blatt used to go sailing. Most of the time he went out alone. He had some rather bright red sails on that boat, but he had some white sails too, hidden. I think he sailed out and was met by another boat and the stuff was passed to him. Then Blatt used to sail into Pixy Cove at a convenient time of day …'

Poirot smiled. 'Yes, at half past one. When everyone is in the dining-room.'
'Yes,' said the chief constable. 'Blatt landed there and put the stuff on that ledge in the cave. Somebody else was going to pick it up later.'

'There was a couple,' said Poirot, 'who came to the island for lunch that day. That would be a way to get the drugs. Summer visitors – they come here for lunch, but walk round the island first. How easy to go down to the beach, pick up the sandwich box and return for lunch at the hotel.'

'Yes, it all sounds likely enough. Now, these gangsters are violent people. If anyone found out what they were doing, they wouldn't think twice about silencing them. So that morning Blatt is in the cave hiding the stuff. Arlena arrives and sees him going into the cave with the box. She asks him about it and he kills her. Then he goes off in his boat as quickly as possible.'

'You think that Blatt is definitely the murderer?'
'It seems the most likely solution. Of course, it's possible that Arlena found out about it earlier, and one of the gangsters fixed an appointment with her and then killed her. Scotland Yard will have a good chance of proving Blatt's connection. Do you think that's the wise thing to do?'

Hercule Poirot was thoughtful. He said at last, 'It may be.'
'Oh, tell me, Poirot, have you got an idea or not?'
Poirot was silent. At last he said, 'I would like to go for a picnic.'

◆

The idea was surprisingly successful. Everyone was doubtful at first and then decided it might not be such a bad idea. Mr Marshall was not asked. He had told them he had to go to Plymouth that day. Mr Blatt joined them, enthusiastically. In addition there was Emily Brewster, the Redferns, Reverend Lane, the Gardeners (who decided not to leave until the next day), Rosamund Darnley and Linda. Major Barry had refused. He said he did not like picnics.

The group met at ten o'clock. Three cars had been ordered. Mr Blatt was loud and cheerful, pretending to be a tourist guide. At the last minute, Rosamund Darnley came down looking worried.

'Linda's not coming. She says she's got a terrible headache. I've given her some pills and she's gone to bed. I think, perhaps, I won't go either.'

'We can't allow that, dear lady,' cried Mr Blatt, taking her arm. 'I've taken you prisoner! You're going to Dartmoor.'

'*I'll* stay with Linda,' said Christine Redfern. 'I don't mind.'

'No, no, you must come, Madame,' said Poirot. 'With a headache it is better to be alone. Come, let us start.'

The cars drove off. They went first to another cave, and had a lot of fun finding the entrance. It was difficult to climb over the big rocks, and Hercule Poirot did not try to do it. He watched while Christine Redfern jumped easily from stone to stone and noticed that her husband was never far from her. Rosamund Darnley and Emily Brewster had joined the search, although Miss Brewster had fallen and slightly hurt herself. Stephen Lane was full of energy, his long thin body turning easily among the rocks. Mr Blatt watched and cheered, and also took photographs.

The Gardeners and Poirot stayed sitting down while Mrs Gardener's voice never stopped, interrupted only occasionally by 'Yes, dear' from her husband.

'... and I always think, and Mr Gardener agrees with me, that photographs can be very annoying. Mr Blatt just comes up to you and takes pictures and, as I said to Mr Gardener, that really is very rude. That photo of all of us sitting on the beach – he didn't ask permission. Then he gave us all copies without asking first. He gave one to you, Monsieur Poirot, I noticed.'

Poirot nodded. 'I value that photograph very much.'

Following Poirot's directions, the group drove to a lovely place near a small river. A narrow bridge crossed the river. Poirot and Mr Gardener helped Mrs Gardener to cross it, to reach a perfect place for a picnic.

Suddenly there was a cry. Emily Brewster was standing in the middle of the bridge, her eyes shut. Poirot and Patrick Redfern rushed to help her.

'Thanks, thanks,' she said. 'I've never been good at crossing running water. I always feel faint. Stupid.'

The picnic began. Everyone was secretly surprised how much they enjoyed it. Here, the world of murder and suspicion did not exist. Even Mr Blatt became calm and quiet, and after lunch he fell happily asleep.

The sun was sinking as they returned along the narrow roads. From the top of the hill, the island looked peaceful and innocent. Mrs Gardener said, 'Thank you, Monsieur Poirot. I feel so calm. It's been wonderful.'

Major Barry came out to greet them. Then Gladys Narracott came out of the hotel too. She was a little breathless. She hurried to Christine Redfern.

'Excuse me, Madam, but I'm worried about Miss Marshall. I took her up some tea just now but I couldn't wake her, and she looks so – so strange.'

Christine looked round, and Poirot was at her side in a moment. His hand under her elbow, he said quietly, 'We will go up and see.'

They hurried up to Linda's room. One look told them both that something was very wrong. She was an odd colour and she was breathing only faintly. Poirot touched her wrist. At the same time he noticed an envelope on the table beside the bed. It was addressed to him.

Mr Marshall came quickly into the room. 'What's the matter with Linda?'

Christine Redfern was crying quietly. Poirot turned and said to Marshall, 'Get a doctor, as quickly as possible. But I'm afraid it may be too late.'

He took the letter with his name on it and opened the envelope. Inside were a few lines of Linda's schoolgirl handwriting.

I think this is the best way. Ask Father to try to forgive me. I killed Arlena. I thought I would be glad – but I'm not. I am very sorry for everything.

◆

They waited in the sitting-room – Marshall, the Redferns, Rosamund Darnley and Hercule Poirot. The door opened and Dr Neasden came in.

'I've done all I can. She may be OK – but there's not much hope.'

'How did she get the stuff?' asked Marshall, his eyes a cold blue.

Neasden opened the door and a servant came in, her eyes red from crying.

'Just tell us again what you saw,' the doctor said.

'I never thought there was anything wrong, although the young lady seemed rather strange. She was in the other lady's room. Mrs Redfern's. She took a little bottle. I thought it was something she'd lent you. She just said, "Oh, this is what I'm looking for …" and went out.'

'My sleeping pills,' whispered Christine. 'I gave her one the night after it happened. She couldn't sleep. I remember her saying, "Will one be enough?" and I said they were very strong – that you should never take more than two.'

Neasden nodded. 'She wanted to be sure – she took six of them.'

'Oh dear,' cried Christine. 'It's my fault. She's dying, and it's my fault …'

'No, you can't blame yourself,' said Kenneth Marshall, 'Linda knew what she was doing. Perhaps – perhaps it was best.' He looked down at the note.

'I don't believe it!' cried Rosamund Darnley. 'I don't believe Linda killed her. Surely it's impossible – on the evidence!'

'Yes,' said Christine, 'it's impossible. I expect she imagined it all.'

The door opened and Weston came in. Dr Neasden took the note from

Marshall's hand and gave it to the chief constable.

He read it and said, 'But this is rubbish. It's impossible, isn't it, Poirot?'

'No,' said Poirot sadly. 'It is not impossible.'

'But I was with her until quarter to twelve,' said Christine.

'Your evidence gave her an alibi, yes. But where does that evidence come from? *Linda Marshall's* own watch. You do not really know the time when you left her – you only know what she told you. You said yourself that the time had gone very fast.' She stared at him, and he continued, 'What were you thinking about on the way back to the hotel?'

'I suppose … I was thinking about leaving here – going away without telling my husband. I was very unhappy.'

'Oh, Christine!' cried Patrick Redfern. 'I know … I know …'

'Exactly,' Poirot's voice interrupted. 'You were thinking hard about something. You probably walked slowly and sometimes stopped to think.'

'How clever!' said Christine. 'It was just like that. I was in a kind of dream until I got to the hotel, and then I hurried in. I thought I was very late, but when I saw the clock in the sitting-room I realised I had plenty of time.'

'Exactly,' said Hercule Poirot again, and he turned to Marshall.

'I must describe some things I found in your daughter's room after the murder. In the fireplace there were some bits of candle, some burnt hair, pieces of cardboard and paper and an ordinary pin. The paper and cardboard might not be important, but the other three things suggested something – especially when I found a book about magic on the book shelf. The book described different ways to kill someone. You make a figure of the person, then you destroy it with fire or push a pin through its heart. Death of the real person follows. I later heard that Linda had been out early that morning and had bought candles, and had seemed embarrassed about them. I had no doubt after that. Linda made a rough figure with the candles, perhaps adding some of Arlena's hair, and then pushed a pin through its heart. Finally she put pieces of cardboard under it and burnt it.

'It was childish and silly, but it showed the desire to kill. But is it possible that Linda Marshall actually killed Arlena? At first, her alibi seemed perfect – but the evidence was given by *Linda herself*. Perhaps she said it was quarter of an hour earlier than it really was. Possibly, when Mrs Redfern left the beach, Linda followed her and then went down the ladder, strangled Arlena and returned up the ladder – all before the boat with Miss Brewster and Mr Redfern appeared. She could then return to the cove, swim and return to the hotel.

'But for that, two things were necessary. She had to know that Arlena would be at Pixy Cove, and she must be strong enough to strangle her. The first is possible – perhaps she wrote a note to Arlena in someone else's handwriting.

And the second – Linda has very large, strong hands. And there is one other thing. Her mother was actually suspected of murder.'

'She was not guilty,' said Kenneth Marshall angrily. 'I am completely certain she was innocent. And I don't believe Linda killed Arlena. It's crazy!'

'Do you believe this letter is not her handwriting?' asked Poirot.

'No,' he said slowly. 'I believe Linda wrote this.'

'If she wrote it,' said Poirot, 'there are only two explanations. Either it is true, or she wrote it to protect someone.'

'You mean me?' said Kenneth Marshall, 'No, that idea is mad. Perhaps Linda realised I was suspected at first. But she knows now that the police have accepted my alibi.'

'But if she knew you were guilty?' said Poirot.

Marshall stared at him and laughed. 'That's crazy.'

'I wonder. There are several possibilities about Mrs Marshall's death. Perhaps she went to meet a blackmailer, and he killed her. Perhaps Pixy Cave was used by gangsters, and she was killed because she found out. Perhaps she was killed by a madman. And there is a fourth possibility – you would make a lot of money from your wife's death, Mr Marshall. I agree it is impossible that you killed your wife – *if you were alone.* But if someone helped you?'

'What do you mean?' The quiet man was shouting at last.

'This crime was not done by one person. It is true that you could not type that letter and at the same time go to the cove – but someone else could type it in your room.' Poirot looked towards Rosamund Darnley. 'Miss Darnley says she left Sunny Ledge at ten minutes past eleven and saw you typing in your room. But at about that time Mr Gardener went up to the hotel to get some wool for his wife. He did not see Miss Darnley. That is rather strange. Either Miss Darnley never left Sunny Ledge, or she had left it much earlier and was typing busily in your room. Another thing – you said that when Miss Darnley looked into your room *you saw her in the mirror.* But on that day your writing table was in the corner of the room and the mirror was between the windows. Later, you moved your typewriter to the table under the mirror – but it was too late. I knew that both you and Miss Darnley had lied.'

'What a clever brain you have!' said Rosamund Darnley.

'But,' said Poirot, more loudly, 'not as clever as the brain of the man who killed Arlena! We all thought that Arlena had gone to meet … who? *Patrick Redfern!* She was not going to meet a blackmailer. Her face told me that. Oh no, she was going to meet a lover. But then a minute later Patrick Redfern appeared and was clearly looking for her.'

'Someone used my name to get her there,' said Patrick Redfern with anger.

'You were clearly upset and surprised by her absence. Almost too clearly, perhaps. I think, Mr Redfern, that she went to Pixy Cove to meet *you*, and that she *did* meet you, and that *you killed her there, as you had planned*.'

'Are you stupid? I was with you on the beach until I went round in the boat with Miss Brewster and found her dead.'

'You killed her after Miss Brewster had gone to get the police. Arlena Marshall was not dead when you got to the beach. She was hiding in the cave.'

'But the body! Miss Brewster and I both saw the body.'

'A body – yes. But not a *dead* body. The *living body* of the woman who helped you – with tanned arms and legs and with her face under a green cardboard hat. Christine helped you in the same way she helped you before, when she "discovered" the body of Alice Corrigan twenty minutes before Alice Corrigan had died – killed by her husband – you!'

'Be careful, Patrick,' said Christine in a cold voice. 'Don't lose your temper.'

'You and Christine were easily recognised by the Surrey police from a group photograph that was taken here. They named you at once as Edward Corrigan and Christine Deverill, the young woman who found the body.'

Redfern stood up. His handsome face was changed – it was red and angry, the face of a killer. He shouted, 'You horrible, stupid little man!'

He threw himself forwards, his fingers stretched out, his voice screaming, as he placed his fingers around Hercule Poirot's throat …

CHAPTER 12

A Very Clever Plan

'Body – the word reminded me of something.
Bodies on the beach all look very similar.'

'One morning,' said Poirot, 'we talked about sun-tanned bodies that looked like meat. I thought then that there is little difference between one body and another. When a woman walks, speaks, laughs, moves – then, yes, she is a person. But when she is lying in the sun – no.

'We spoke of evil that day – *evil under the sun*, as Reverend Lane said. Reverend Lane is affected by evil, but he did not know exactly where it was. To him, evil was in the person of Arlena Marshall, and almost everyone agreed with him. But to me, although evil was present, it was not in Arlena. She was beautiful and men turned to look at her, so people thought she was the type of woman who destroyed lives. But I had a different opinion. She liked men. Men cared for her easily but they got tired of her. One man was divorced because of her, but refused to marry her. Then Mr Marshall asked her to marry him. To a shy man like Mr Marshall, public difficulties would be terrible – this explains his love and pity for his first wife. He married her and found he had been right about her character. After her death, when another beautiful woman's problems became public, Marshall saved her too. Arlena did *not* deserve him – she was stupid, mindless. But, long after he stopped loving her, Marshall still felt sorry for her. She was like a child who could not grow up.

'I saw that a certain type of man was interested in Arlena. Patrick Redfern, with his confidence, his attractiveness, was that type – the adventurer who lives from women. I was sure that *he* was the evil one, not Arlena.

'Arlena had recently been left a large sum of money by an admirer who had not had time to get tired of her. Miss Brewster spoke of a young man who had been "destroyed" by Arlena, but a letter from him actually thanked *her* for money. Redfern made her give him large sums. Unprotected women are easily used by that type of man, and he usually escapes. But if there is a husband, a brother, or a father, things often get unpleasant for the criminal. When Mr Marshall found out, Redfern might expect trouble. This did not worry him, because he planned to kill her when necessary. He had already murdered one person – he had married a young woman, calling himself Corrigan, and did well financially from her death.

'He was helped by the woman who pretended to be his wife, and of whom he is truly fond. She was cool, unemotional, but completely loyal and a clever actress. Christine Redfern played a part, the "poor little wife" – weak, helpless, intelligent, not sporty. She told us that she could not go out in the sun, that heights made her faint. Nearly everyone called her a "little woman". She was actually as tall as Arlena, but with very small hands and feet. She said she had been a schoolteacher, and seemed interested in books, not sport. Actually, she had worked as a *sports teacher,* and she was a very active young woman who could climb like a cat and run like the wind.

'The crime itself was perfectly planned and timed. It was, as I said before, a very clever plan. The timing was excellent. First, there were the opening scenes – one on the cliff ledge when they knew I could hear them, a conversation between a jealous wife and her husband. Later, she played the same scene with me. At the time it did not seem *real* – because it was *not* real. Then came the day of the crime. It was a fine day – very necessary. Redfern went out very early, by the balcony door. Under his towel he hid a green Chinese hat, like the one that Arlena usually wore. He went across the island, down the ladder and hid it behind some rocks. Part One.

'The evening before, he had arranged a rendezvous with Arlena. She had agreed to go round to Pixy Cove early. Nobody went there in the morning. Redfern was going to meet her there. If she heard anyone coming down the ladder or if a boat appeared she was going to hide inside Pixy Cave and wait. Part Two.

'Christine went to Linda's room, when she thought Linda would be having her morning swim. She changed Linda's watch, moving it forward twenty minutes. Of course, Linda might notice her watch was wrong, but it did not really matter. Christine's real alibi was the size of her hands – she could not be the murderer. Then in Linda's room she noticed the book about magic, open at a certain page. She read it, and then Linda came in and dropped a package of candles. She realised what was in Linda's mind. It gave her some new ideas. The first idea had been to make Kenneth Marshall look guilty – that is why his pipe was taken, and a piece of it was placed under the ladder.

'When Linda returned, Christine easily arranged a trip together to Gull Cove. She then returned to her own room, took a bottle of tanning oil from a suitcase and put the false tan all over her body. Then she threw the empty bottle out of the window, nearly hitting Emily Brewster, who was swimming. Part Three.

'Christine then put on a white swimsuit, and over it some trousers and a blouse which hid her recently tanned arms and legs. At 10.15 Arlena left for her meeting. A minute or two later, Patrick Redfern came down and looked annoyed. Christine's job was easy. Hiding her own watch, she asked Linda at twenty-five past eleven what time it was. Linda replied that it was quarter to twelve, and then went down to the sea. When Linda's back was turned,

Christine picked up the girl's watch and changed it back to the correct time. Then she hurried up the cliff path and across to the ladder, pulled off the trousers and blouse and pushed them and her drawing things behind a rock. Then she climbed down the ladder, fast.

'Arlena was on the beach below, wondering why Patrick was so late. She saw or heard someone on the ladder, had a careful look, and saw that inconvenient person – the wife! She hurried into Pixy Cave.

'Christine took the hat from its hiding place. It had some false red hair pinned to it. She lay face down with the hat and hair covering her head and neck. A minute or two later, the boat with Patrick Redfern and Emily Brewster came round the corner. Remember, it was *Patrick* who bent down and examined the body, *Patrick* who was shocked – destroyed – by the death of his lady love! His witness had been carefully chosen. He knew Miss Brewster did not like heights; she would not try to go up the ladder. She would leave the cove by boat, and Patrick would stay with the body. Miss Brewster rowed away to get the police. Christine, when the boat had disappeared, jumped up and cut the hat into pieces with the scissors which Patrick had brought. She then pushed them under her swimsuit, climbed the ladder fast, pulled on her trousers and blouse and ran back to the hotel. There was just time to have a quick bath to wash off the false brown tan, and to put on her tennis dress. She did one other thing. She burnt the pieces of green cardboard hat in Linda's fireplace. She added a page of a notebook, so it appeared that a *notebook*, not a hat, had been burnt. As she had guessed, Linda had already tried magic – the candle and the pin showed that.

'Then she went down to the tennis court, arriving last but not hurrying.

'While this was happening, Patrick had gone to the cave. Arlena had seen nothing and heard little. She had stayed hidden. But now Patrick was calling her. She came out, his hands closed around her neck, and that was the end of poor foolish, beautiful Arlena Marshall.'

For a moment there was silence, then Rosamund Darnley said, 'Yes, but you haven't told us how *you* found out what happened.'

'From the beginning, it seemed to me that *the most likely person* had killed Arlena Marshall. And the most likely person was Patrick Redfern. He was the kind of man who takes a woman's money and cuts her throat too. Who was Arlena going to meet? By the evidence of her face, her smile, her words to me – *Patrick Redfern*. And therefore it was probably Patrick who killed her.

'But that was impossible. Redfern was on the beach and with Miss Brewster until the body was discovered. So I looked for other solutions. Perhaps her husband had killed her – with Miss Darnley's help. (They too had both lied about something.) Or perhaps she was killed by drug smugglers, or by a madman, or by her husband's daughter. The last idea seemed at one time to be the real solution. Linda's behaviour in her first interview was very important. A later interview made me sure of one thing – Linda thought she was guilty.'

'You mean she imagined she had actually killed Arlena?' asked Rosamund.

'Yes. She read that book on magic and she half believed it. She hated Arlena. She made the figure, pushed the pin through its heart – *and that same day Arlena died*. Naturally, she believed that she had killed her.'

'Oh, poor child!' cried Rosamund, 'And I thought – I imagined ...'

'I know what you thought,' said Poirot. 'Actually your behaviour frightened Linda even more. She believed that she really had killed Arlena and that you knew it. Then Christine Redfern introduced the idea of sleeping pills, showing her a speedy and painless way to pay for her crime. When Mr Marshall's alibi was proved, there had to be a new person to suspect. She and Patrick did not know about the drugs. They chose Linda.'

'What an evil woman!' said Rosamund Darnley.

'Yes, you are right. She is a cold-blooded and cruel woman. I was in great difficulty. Was Linda guilty only of trying magic, or had her hate carried her to actual murder? I tried to make her tell me, but it was no good. At that moment, Weston was moving towards the drug smuggling idea. I had pieces of a puzzle – the scissors, a bottle, a bath – all harmless things, but important. They *had to* mean something. I went back again to my first idea – that Patrick Redfern had murdered Arlena. Did anything support that? Yes, a large sum of Arlena's

money had disappeared. Who had that money? Patrick Redfern. She was easily robbed, but not the type to be blackmailed. She was not good enough at keeping a secret. The blackmailer story had never seemed true to me. Who had heard that conversation about blackmail? Patrick Redfern's wife. Why? The answer came to me suddenly. To explain the disappearance of Arlena's money!

'Patrick and Christine Redfern worked together. Christine was not strong enough to strangle her. No, it was Patrick – but that was impossible! We knew about every minute of his time until the body was found. Body – the word reminded me of something. Bodies on the beach *all look very similar*. Patrick Redfern and Emily Brewster had seen a *body*. Perhaps it was not Arlena's body? The head was hidden by the great Chinese hat.

'But there was only one dead body – Arlena's. So, could it be a living body? Whose? Was there a woman who would help Redfern? Of course – his wife. But she was a weak, pale-skinned woman. Yes, but you can get a tan from a bottle. I had one of my puzzle pieces. And afterwards a bath, to wash off the tan before she played tennis. The scissors? To cut up that cardboard hat, and in the rush the scissors were left behind – the only thing the murderers forgot.

'But where was Arlena all this time? That again was perfectly clear. Either Rosamund or Arlena had been in Pixy Cave – I could smell the perfume. It was certainly not Rosamund. So it was Arlena, hiding.

'When Emily Brewster went off in the boat, Patrick was alone on the beach and he had the opportunity to murder Arlena. She was killed after quarter to twelve, but the doctor was only interested in the earliest possible time. He was told by Miss Brewster that Arlena was dead by quarter to twelve.'

'There were two more things. I needed to prove that Christine had two opportunities to change Linda's watch. It was easy. She had been alone in Linda's room that morning. Linda said she was afraid she was going to be late, but when she got downstairs the sitting-room clock said twenty-five past ten. The second opportunity was easy – she could change the watch back again when Linda turned her back and went to swim. Then there was the ladder. Christine had always said she couldn't stand heights. Another lie.

'I had my picture now – each piece fitted beautifully. But I could not prove it. Then an idea came to me. It was a confident crime. This was possibly not the first time that Redfern had killed. If he was already a murderer, I was sure he had used the same method. I asked for a list of similar murders. The result pleased me. The death of Nellie Parsons might or might not be Redfern's work, but Alice Corrigan's death was exactly what I was looking for. The same method. Changing times – a murder that happened not *before* people thought it had happened, but *afterwards*. A body that was "discovered" at quarter past four. A husband with an alibi until twenty-five past four.

'What really happened? People said that when Edward Corrigan arrived at the café and found his wife wasn't there, he *went outside*. Actually, he ran to the meeting, killed her and returned to the café. A sports teacher walked to the police station to report the crime. The police doctor examined the body at quarter to six. In the same way as now, the time of death was not questioned.

'I made one final test. I arranged our little trip to Dartmoor. Miss Brewster became faint while crossing a narrow bridge over water, but Christine Redfern ran across with no problem. If she lied once, all the other lies were possible. The Surrey police had already named the people in the photograph. I made Redfern feel safe, and then I tried to make him lose his self-control. When he knew he was recognised as Corrigan, he went completely mad.

'That,' said Hercule Poirot with importance, 'was very dangerous – but I am glad I did it. I succeeded! I did not suffer needlessly.'

'Well, Monsieur Poirot,' said Mrs Gardener, 'it's been wonderful. Imagine! My wool and our conversation helped! That makes me so excited, and I'm sure Mr Gardener feels the same – don't you, Odell?'

'Yes, dear,' said Mr Gardener.

'Mr Gardener helped me too,' said Hercule Poirot. 'I wanted the opinion of a sensible man about Mrs Marshall. I asked him what he thought of her.'

'And what did you say, Odell?'

'Well, dear, I never thought much of her, you know.'

'I thought she was a bit stupid. I said so to Mr Gardener – didn't I, Odell?'

'Yes, dear,' said Mr Gardener.

Linda Marshall sat with Hercule Poirot on Gull Cove.

'Of course I'm glad I didn't die. But I did *plan* to kill her.'

'It's not the same thing,' said Hercule Poirot firmly. 'The wish and the action are two different things. You would not really kill. You made a figure and pushed pins into it – it was childish, yes, but useful too. You took the hate out of yourself and put it into that little figure. Afterwards, even before you heard of her death, you felt better, happier, didn't you?' Linda nodded. 'So you must decide not to hate your father's next wife.'

'Rosamund? I don't mind her. She's *sensible*.'

◆

Marshall said, 'Did you have the crazy idea that I'd killed Arlena?'

'I suppose I was a fool,' said Rosamund, rather embarrassed. 'But I never knew what you really felt about Arlena. I didn't know if you accepted her as she was, or if you just believed in her blindly. If it was that, and you suddenly found out about Redfern, you might go mad with anger. I've heard stories about you. You're very quiet but you're rather frightening sometimes.'

'So you thought I took her by the throat and strangled her?'

'Yes, that's exactly what I thought. And your alibi didn't seem good enough.

That's when I decided to help – I said I'd seen you typing. And when you said you'd seen me, I was sure you'd done it. That, and Linda's odd behaviour.'

'Don't you realise? I said I'd seen you in the mirror to support *your* story.'

Rosamund stared at him. 'Do you mean you thought I'd killed your wife?'

'Well, you nearly killed that boy about that dog. You held on to his throat.'

'But that was years ago. What motive did you think I had to kill Arlena?' He looked away. 'Ken, what a big head you have! Did you think I killed her to help you? Or – did you think I killed her because I wanted you myself?'

'Not at all. But you know what you said that day – about Linda – and you seemed to care about me. I'm not good with words, but I'd like to make one thing clear. I didn't love Arlena – only a little, at first. I didn't enjoy living with her, but I was very sorry for her. She was such a fool – crazy about men – and they always left her and behaved badly to her. I didn't want to make it worse. I'd married her and I had to look after her. I think she was grateful.'

'It's all right, Ken. I understand now.'

Without looking at her, Kenneth Marshall carefully filled his pipe. 'You're – quite good at understanding, Rosamund.'

'Are you going to ask me to marry you, or are you going to wait six months?'

Marshall's pipe dropped from his lips and crashed onto the rocks below.

'Oh, that's the second pipe I've lost here. And I haven't got another one. How did you know I'd decided six months was the right time?'

'Because it *is* the right time. But I'd rather have a definite decision now, please. You might meet another sad female and rush to save her.'

'You're going to be the sad female this time,' he laughed. 'You're going to give up your business and we're going to live in the country.'

'Oh, my dear,' said Rosamund softly. 'I've wanted to live in the country with you all my life. Now – it's going to happen …'

1 Work with five or six other students. Discuss what each of these people thought (or pretended to think) about Arlena Marshall before she died. Then play the parts of the characters, and have a conversation about her.

What do you think of Mrs Marshall?

2 Work with one or two other students. Choose *either* Patrick and Christine Redfern *or* Rosamund, Kenneth and Linda and imagine their lives during the few months after the end of the story. Make notes on your discussion, then tell the class.

a How have their lives changed?

b Where do they live now?

c How do they feel about each other?

d What are their plans for the future?

How was Arlena Marshall killed? Put these events in the correct order (1–10). Then complete the report. Use details from the story, and write in a formal style.

a Christine climbed down the ladder. ......

b Patrick killed Arlena. ......

c Poirot saw Arlena getting into a boat. ...1...

d Arlena hid in the cave. ......

e Christine lay down on the beach. ......

f Arlena went to Pixy Cove. ......

g Christine went up the ladder. ......

h Emily went to get the police. ......

i Patrick and Emily saw 'the body'. ......

j Patrick called Arlena's name. ......

Hercule Poirot arrived at the beach at 10 a.m. He saw Mrs Marshall getting into a boat. We now know that she ...

Many films have been made, for television and the cinema, of Agatha Christie's murder mysteries.

1 Work in pairs or small groups and imagine that you are going to film a murder story. Note down your decisions about the film in the table below.

Title of film:

Time:

Place:

Person killed:

Murderer:

Motive:

Murderer's alibi:

Detective(s):

Other main characters:

2 Now discuss each of the main characters. Write short descriptions in note form, including information about:

• age and appearance • style of clothes • job • personality • family background

....

....

....

....

....

....

....

....

3 Imagine that you are going to play one of the characters in the film. Complete this email to a friend.

To: Jo

Subject:

Hi! How are you? I'm really excited because I've just got a part in a new film.

It's a murder mystery film called ....

.... I'm playing ...., who is ....

....

....

This is what happens in the story: ....

....

....

....

That's all I'm going to tell you. You'll find out the rest when you watch the film!

See you soon!

....

4 **Now work with your friends and design a poster for your film. Include:**

- the title of the film and the names of the main actors
- a few words or sentences that introduce the story
- what newspaper reporters have written about the film
- a picture, or ideas for the picture